SUCCESS WITH
Biscuit Joiners

D0129534

SUCCESS WITH
Biscuit Joiners

ANTHONY BAILEY

GUILD OF MASTER CRAFTSMAN PUBLICATIONS LTD

684.083
BA 1

First published 2005 by
Guild of Master Craftsman Publications Ltd,
166 High Street, Lewes,
East Sussex BN7 1XU

Text © Anthony Bailey, 2005
Copyright in the Work © Guild of Master Craftsman
Publications Ltd, 2005

$15.96

ISBN 1 86108 431 5
A catalogue record of this book is available from the British Library.

All rights reserved

The right of Anthony Bailey to be identified as the author of this work
has been asserted in accordance with the Copyright Designs and Patents
Act 1988, Sections 77 and 78.

All trademarks are the property of their respective owners. Many of the
designations used by manufacturers and sellers to distinguish their
products are claimed as trademarks. Where GMC was aware of a
trademark claim, they have been printed in capitals or initial capitals.
No such use, or the use of any trade name, is intended to convey
endorsement or other affiliation with the book.

No part of this publication may be reproduced, stored in a retrieval
system, or transmitted in any form or by any means without the prior
permission of the publishers and copyright owner.

The publishers and author can accept no legal responsibility for any
consequences arising from the application of information, advice or
instructions given in this publication.

Production Manager: Hilary MacCallum
Managing Editor: Gerrie Purcell
Editor: Rachel Netherwood

Photography: Anthony Bailey
Cover design: Oliver Prentice
Book design: Ian Hunt

Typefaces: Palatino and Frutiger

Colour origination. Wyndeham Graphics
Printed and bound: Kyodo Printing, Singapore

HELENA COLLEGE OF TECHNOLOGY LIBRARY
1115 NORTH ROBERTS
HELENA. MONTANA

Acknowledgements

To my wife Patsy and the children – Alex 16, Lucy 14, Amber 12 and Francis 10. It hasn't been quite so much of a trial for them second time around I'm glad to say.

I wish to thank Gerrie Purcell for giving me the 'green flag', James Evans for essential guidance and Rachel Netherwood who edited my book for me, as well as the book designer Ian Hunt. Since I am a professional photographer and depend on the highest quality of transparency processing I would like to thank everyone at Spectrum Photographic of Hove. I would also like to thank all those manufacturers (too many to mention all by name) who have been happy to supply biscuit joiners for me to play with! A book is very much a joint effort by everyone, not just the author so my apologies to anyone who may have been unintentionally left off the list.

Contents

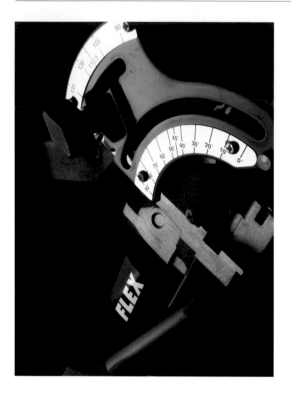

Part 2:

Techniques

Part 3:

Projects

Introduction

Some years ago I worked for an interior design company as a cabinetmaker. At that point I didn't have vast experience in pure woodworking as I had started in business as an antique restorer, so this was a valuable addition to my education. One partner of the interior design company was a woodworker and designer himself and he owned an old Bosch swing-down model which was suffering from age and heavy use. It certainly wasn't a good advert for biscuit jointing and he had little regard for it, especially as he had just leased a workshop full of brand-new machinery. One day however, we were faced with the fact that one lone strip of moulding, out of many we had produced, had not been grooved on the spindle moulder as it should have been and the massive office desk to which it was to be fixed was overdue for delivery – enter the knackered joiner!

What happened next was a revelation. In just five minutes the joiner was set up for use, strike marks for the joints made and the joints cut! All that remained was to glue and cramp the errant strip in place.

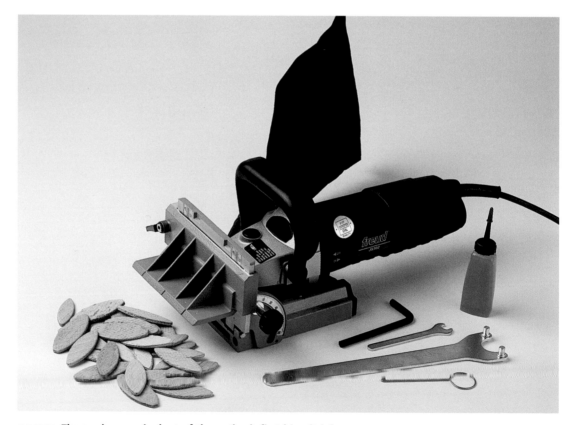

ABOVE **The modern equivalent of the author's first biscuit joiner.**

ABOVE A Flex Porter Cable joiner.

The speed and ease of use amazed me and struck a chord – what simpler, more effective and precise way of fitting wood together could there possibly be?

I was determined to discover more and with my next pay packet I bought a cheap Freud model. With my usual enthusiasm and a large dollop of ignorance I set about using it for all kinds of cabinet work and in many different situations. Indeed I discovered it could easily be pushed beyond its intended limit, to do other less obvious but equally useful things.

The biscuit joiner is often still my first port of call when embarking on a project and without a shadow of a doubt I would thoroughly recommend the acquisition of one to any woodworker, no matter what level of skill or experience. Apart from the router, the joiner is the perfect place to start from; it makes simple jobs even simpler and complex ones possible.

My own, self-taught knowledge of the biscuit joiner and the satisfaction of using such a brilliantly simple tool has made writing this book relatively easy, I hope that both beginners and advanced woodworkers will find much of interest and enjoyment in this book about woodworking's best kept 'open secret' – the biscuit joiner!

Part 1:
Equipment

Part 1:
Equipment

1:1 The biscuit joiner

It is hard to emphasize enough just how simple a concept the biscuit, and the associated biscuit joiner, is and yet at the same time how much further you can push the concept and get it to do much more than cut a few slots. It appeals to me because it is so simple and so versatile. There are now more models on the market than ever and prices vary from cheap to expensive so there is no reason for not being able to afford one. It is the tool I reach for first before any other power tool because I can saw out board, joint it and even decorate it a little with just one machine and it can go with me anywhere, including on site where its compact and easy-to-use nature make it ideal. Beech biscuits and PVA (polyvinyl acetate) glue are cheap too, making it an all-round piece of 'dream kit'. It is the perfect machine for the professional and enthusiast alike.

What does it do?

The answer to this question can be short or long, as you will find out in successive pages of this book. To keep it brief for the time being, suffice it to say that the original aim of its inventor, Hermann Steiner, owner of a Swiss joinery company, was to create a simple, cheap and easy way of jointing wood without the need for great skill, and that is exactly what he managed to achieve. The biscuit joiner probably wouldn't exist if it wasn't for his efforts; his company Lamello AG (*lamella* is the Latin word for thin plate, scale, layer or film, usually applied to bone or tissue – *Oxford English Dictionary* definition) is still at the forefront of design and production of biscuit joiners and specialized allied products (mainly for trade users), while other manufacturers have been busy developing their own joiners intended for more general use.

The joiner has a motor of between 550 and 750 watt input power, right-angle gearing (like an angle grinder), a mini-sawblade of 4in (100mm) diameter, a housing to cover the blade, a means of pushing the blade out of the housing and safely retracting after the cut is made, and a means of setting the depth of cut. There is also some kind of adjustable fence fitted on for guidance.

The standard biscuits (sometimes termed splines or plates) that it uses come in three regular sizes: 0, 10 and 20, which are stamped out of fine-grained beech wood and are ⁵⁄₃₂in (4mm) thick, the same as the joiner blade. However, there are several tricks needed to make the biscuit work properly: 1) the beech biscuits are compressed during the stamping so that they will swell once wet with glue inside the joint; 2) they have a hatched pattern which makes them grip the sides of each slot when they swell, and 3) most importantly, the grain runs at 45° so that once the joint is closed the biscuits are so strong they cannot snap, which is what would happen if the grain ran along the direction of the joint. It's a simple concept, but it must have taken some thought and careful development to achieve a proper functioning joint that worked every single time!

This in essence is what the biscuit joiner (or spline joiner; jointer in the UK) and the humble beech biscuit are all about. However, as a taster for later chapters, here are some of the weird and wonderful things your joiner can be asked to do: join solid timber and manufactured boards; create entire furniture carcasses; make joints that substitute for many of the conventional woodworking joints;

saw boards to size; make knock-down furniture; add various functional features to your furniture, such as sliding doors or drawer pulls; add decorative detail and even repair old or antique table tops! So you see, the joiner may be simple but it is never dull; all the possibilities are out there!

ABOVE A very simple but effective jointing concept.

Anatomy of a biscuit joiner

All biscuit joiners have features in common which are described here. The model you choose may vary from this one.

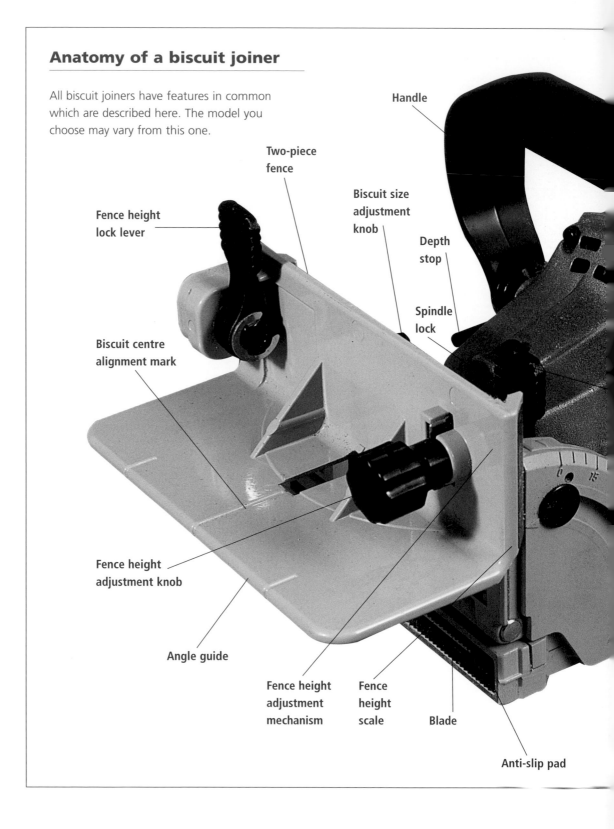

Handle

Two-piece fence

Biscuit size adjustment knob

Depth stop

Spindle lock

Fence height lock lever

Biscuit centre alignment mark

Fence height adjustment knob

Angle guide

Fence height adjustment mechanism

Fence height scale

Blade

Anti-slip pad

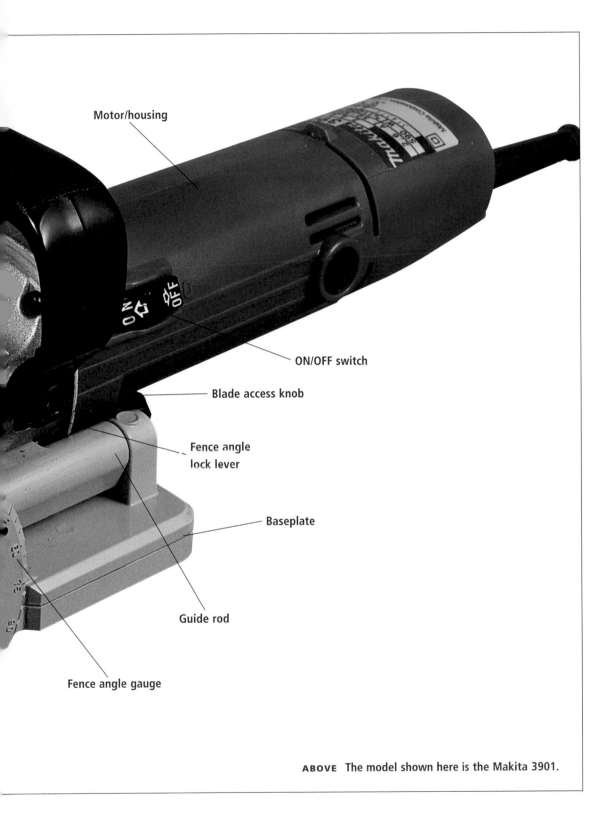

Motor/housing

ON/OFF switch

Blade access knob

Fence angle
lock lever

Baseplate

Guide rod

Fence angle gauge

ABOVE The model shown here is the Makita 3901.

FOCUS ON:

Plunge and
swing-down
body types

FOCUS ON:

Plunge and swing-down body types

The basic pattern for the joiner, as determined by Lamello's design and copied by virtually everybody else, might be described as the 'plunge' type – which is to say that you grip the motor body and push the running blade straight into the workpiece. The alternative swing-down type is just that: the motor hinges on a pivot and the blade swings into the workpiece in an arc. This sort is more suited to board sawing since the motor body can be swung down behind the blade allowing it to be pushed along easily; the plunge type has the motor above the blade and the workpiece and is therefore less suitable for this operation. As there is only one swing-down machine currently on the market, the choice of which type to go for is more or less made for you.

RIGHT A Makita
plunge joiner.

RIGHT The
DeWalt swing-
down model.

Features

Here are some of the features to look out for on a joiner and their relative importance to you as a purchaser of a new machine.

ABOVE **The motor core exposed.**

Motor

The motor wattage isn't critical, as plunging can be done slowly or quite quickly but you won't really miss the lack of extra wattage – even cheap machines are powerful. Not all motor wattage figures give a good picture of actual output power, which is what really counts.

Switch

These tend to be the push-on, flick-off type which means they go to the off position quite easily for safety. Others may need to be held in the on position against spring pressure – let go and they switch off. Whatever type you go for is a matter of personal preference. Electronics are not normally fitted, as joiners only operate at one cutting speed. Apart from a damaged mains lead, the switch is the most likely fail point on your machine.

ABOVE **The switch is fairly easy to change if it wears out.**

Motor brushes

In common with all power tools, joiners have carbon brushes (blocks) which conduct electricity to the motor core; the friction eventually wears the brushes down and then they need replacing. Easy access to them is an advantage, though the short work cycles for slotting wood should mean this won't be necessary for a long time.

Right-angle gear head

This converts the direction of the power from the motor through 90° so that the blade is presented to the work in the correct attitude. Some people unkindly describe biscuit joiners as being based on angle grinders (which is half true and the noise of the gearing is irritatingly similar!). Some models are quieter than others.

RIGHT Short 'work cycles' should mean the brushes won't need to be changed for a long time.

RIGHT Right-angle gearing can be noisy.

LEFT Different blade
types but essentially
the same result.

Blade

Joiner blades, apart from those in heavy
industrial static setups, are all 4in (100mm)
in diameter, though the DeWalt swing-
down model can also take a ply cutting
blade which is slightly larger. Not all
machines have the same size bore hole
in the middle so be careful when selecting
replacement blades. The number of teeth,
which are always TCT (tungsten carbide),
can vary too: six teeth per blade is the
optimum but cheaper machines may have
only four, while the now-defunct Lamello
Dynamic cordless had just two. Mostly they
have an anti-kickback design which means
there is a hump in the blade body just ahead
of each tooth; this prevents too large and
rapid a bite being taken out of the wood
which can result in the machine jumping
away from the workpiece, thus hazarding
the operator and spoiling the work. The
most expensive blades may have 'scoring'
tips on the blades for neat cutting of the
wood fibres or they may have disposable
tips for very demanding trade use.

Handgrip

All plunge type joiners have a top, loop-
shaped handgrip, which can be quite large
and easy to get hold of or it can be too
close to the gear housing and result in
scraped knuckles. It exists mainly to carry
the machine around – when machining
it is often better to grip the top of the
fence instead. If it can be swung down
or removed, this helps when working in
tight corners.

ABOVE Handgrip and general ergonomics are a
matter of personal taste.

Slide mechanism

This applies to the plunge machine and is normally one of two types: a) a casting fixed to the gear head which slides in grooves in a big cast blade housing that also forms the base (see below), or b) two chromed rods sliding in a cast housing which are in turn fixed to the blade housing (see right). Either way the slide mechanism must slide freely and smoothly against the pressure of the return springs which are needed to keep the dangerous blade sheathed when out of the wood. More expensive machines may have one part of the sliding assembly nickel-plated

ABOVE Makita rod-type slide mechanism.

or chromed because the use of two aluminium alloy components sliding together causes 'wiping' (i.e. the surface of the metal changes as it rubs against itself) which results in roughness, then friction and resultant wear. Regular lubrication of the sliding assembly is important.

Blade housing

This is the most important part from the safety point of view, however you do need access to the inside for blade changing. On the Freud it is a matter of unhooking the return springs with a wire hook contrivance after removing the faceplate, thus exposing the blade fully as it slides right out. The Makita, which is a more expensive machine, has a rather nice lift-up baseplate with a knob to lock it shut, thus giving easy instant access. Some joiners need two spanners for undoing the blade securing nut while others have a push button on the top of the housing

ABOVE Lamello Top 20 slide housing.

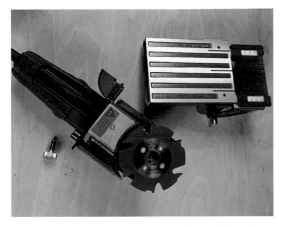

ABOVE The Lamello has a slide-off blade housing held in place with one knob.

to lock the shaft so that only one spanner is needed. The faceplate and baseplate on the housing should be cleanly and accurately machined at 90° to each other for repeatable precision when slotting.

Fence/fall-front

Fences come in different patterns, most commonly those that are fixed at 90° and 45° or alternatively are fully adjustable down to 90°. However, machines are increasingly being fitted with fences that go well beyond 90° to an acute 135°, as on the Draper (ex Ryobi) and the Flex Porter Cable. This has distinct advantages if you intend on doing a lot of mitres, because the wood can be neatly trapped between fence and faceplate for safer, more precise jointing. Some machines even have geared fences for precise setting such as on the DeWalt. Lamellos have a fixed-angle fence and an adjustable fall-front instead, which means the front plate swings down with the fence attached if needed.

ABOVE One type of fall-front, which stops at 90°. Others are more extreme.

Dust extraction

All joiners have extraction ports and often come with a dustbag. Dustbags are optimistic really, rather like trying to catch an elephant's droppings in a teacup – so prodigious is the output of a joiner that it can't be contained for long in a small bag. A proper vacuum extractor is vital for regular use, preferably with auto-power tool switching. This means the extractor only turns on when you switch on the power tool and shuts off after a delay period to allow the hose to clear of dust.

The dust ports on joiners are usually rather small or have a projection inside to prevent fingers being poked into the path of a running blade. What stops meat going in, by the same token stops wood coming out and blockages are common, especially with the long curly shavings produced by timbers such as oak or pine. There isn't really an answer to this one.

Depth stop

Jointing wouldn't be possible without accurate repeatable depth setting. Since there are three standard biscuit sizes, this is the minimum number of depth stages you need to be able to set (although there is also a slimmer 'mini biscuit' and a super-size biscuit made by Lamello). Being able to groove or saw also requires different depth settings, especially at the maximum depth of cut possible. Even if manufacturers may not officially like their

ABOVE Alternative dustspouts for use with or without extraction.

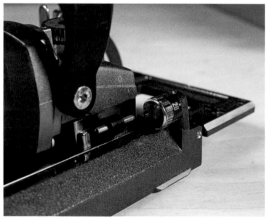

ABOVE The depth stop usually has at least six settings. In addition the fine adjuster can be altered to suit needs.

The biscuit joiner

machines being used as saws they still fit depth turrets which generally give five or six settings, including one that allows a ¾–⅞in (19–22mm) cut depth. A fine adjuster is also provided but if this is altered you need to return it to the original position so your slots don't come out too shallow – or worse – too deep! Do some test cuts to ascertain the correct setting first.

Scales

Most power tools have few, if any scales; those that exist are not very reliable. In theory the joiner needs scales more than most machines. The protractor scales marked on fences or fall-fronts are OK and there may be click stops for commonly used angles. Fence height adjustment is another matter; generally it is better to measure the machine's settings with a small steel engineer's rule and do test cuts as well to confirm the settings. Only the most expensive machines have reliable scales.

Additional features

There are several features which are peculiar to the swing-down type of joiner; these are covered in the gallery in chapter 1:3 and also in chapter 2:9.

ABOVE On an expensive machine the scales should be reliable enough to use.

1:2 Safety

We all recognize the importance of safety but in reality it is often seen as inconvenient and expensive, with itchy, hot facemasks, uncomfortable ear defenders and awkward boots or garments. There are choices we need to make so that woodworking is carried out in as safe a fashion as possible. It starts with the planning of a job and how each operation is to be carried out. Fortunately the biscuit joiner is a pretty safe machine to work with so long as you use your common sense. The retractable blade housing ensures that the blade is only exposed (in the wood) for just as long as the tool is plunged. Keeping the blade sharp, using anti-slip devices and even making use of static setups all contribute to a safe, enjoyable and satisfying experience with the biscuit joiner. Finally, the importance of using a proper vacuum extractor cannot be over-emphasized, as the joiner produces prodigious amounts of waste.

Workshop safety

In my first book, *Routing for Beginners* (published by GMC Publications), I covered workshop safety quite thoroughly, because routers work particularly well in a dedicated environment. Whereas the router benefits from being mounted on a decent-size router table, the biscuit joiner is almost exclusively a freestanding power tool that can work anywhere, except for the certain static setups mentioned in chapter 2:8. The router more easily forms a kind of 'machining centre' for a workshop.

ABOVE A tidy workshop is much easier to work in.

So the decision whether to turn your shed or garage into a decent workshop environment is not crucial. Nevertheless, a pleasant, clean, well-lit environment is not only good to work in, it also makes for improved safety.

Make sure any existing building is sound- and leakproof. Carry out any draft-proofing or other repairs. If necessary, fit larger windows for better daylight illumination. Consider installing insulation and a second inner-skin wall-lining using sterling board or thin shuttering ply. Ensure the electrical circuitry is safe and up to date. If there is none you will need to install a supply sufficient for lighting and several power sockets, which is a job for a qualified electrician. If the floor is concrete it will be possible to lay sheets of expanded polystyrene with ply or interlocking chipboard flooring over it for an insulated working area, so that your feet won't freeze in winter!

Storage

Flammable liquids or gases must be properly stored. A can of petrol for a mower, for example, should be sealed to prevent ignition caused by sparking motors or switches. Don't allow junk to pile up – keep everything properly stored and well organized on shelves. It's easy to say, I know, but really essential. Always sweep up and vacuum dust and chippings at the end of a session. Working in a tidy environment is more comfortable and enjoyable too.

Heating

Heating is always a bit problematic. Any source of open flame heating can cause sudden combustion of dust or chippings, so an oil-filled heater or a radiator fed off your home's central heating may be the answer. Consult your local dealer for more information on suitable models. A fire extinguisher should also be considered, as speed is essential if you are to have any hope of dealing with a fire. Choose a type suitable for electrical fires – i.e. not water-filled.

Machine safety

All power tools sold in the UK come with safety instructions that comply with EC safety directives (US-sold machines must comply with the American equivalent). Manufacturers want you to use your tools properly and safely; if you have a good experience using their machines you might buy something else made by them in the future, so safety sells! Read these instructions – they cover obvious points like: don't work in the rain or a wet environment; no long hair, loose clothing or jewellery; keep children and pets away from the working area. However it is a very basic and important first step that these rules should be enforced for everyone's benefit.

FOCUS ON:

Start-up basics

FOCUS ON:

Start-up basics

Take your new biscuit joiner out of its box and check nothing is broken or missing. Familiarize yourself with the machine with the power off using the handbook as a guide. Most importantly, the blade housing must be able to retract and spring back very easily and the blade must turn freely.

Once you are sure all is well, take a suitable piece of board, cramp it down properly, and set the fence so the blade is roughly centred on the edge of the board. Hold the machine in place with the fence and faceplate pressed firmly and squarely on the board but without the blade being plunged at all. Switch on, allow the motor a couple of seconds to come up to speed and plunge. Allow the blade to retract by slackening your arm pressure and switch off.

RIGHT A neat-fitting boiler suit, ear defenders, extraction hose and workpiece cramped firmly in the vice make for safe working.

Dos and don'ts

Do use the joiner in the correct condition as supplied by the manufacturer; never be tempted to alter the way it works. In particular, do nothing to impede the operation of the spring return on the blade housing. On occasions where this has been attempted, the results have been predictably disastrous and could have caused serious injury.

Do maintain the blade in good condition. Although the blades are TCT (tungsten carbide) tipped they do eventually wear if a lot of slotting is done and especially if used for sawing. It is important to keep the blade tips clean if they get blackened or coated with dust and resin, as this will stop the blade from cutting efficiently and also impose more strain on the motor. Keeping a separate blade or jointer for sawing is a good idea, thus ensuring the best blade is used for biscuit slotting.

Don't work with both the joiner and the workpiece loose – i.e. uncramped. I met a well-known woodworker who confessed that he had tried jointing through two thin sheets of ply, more or less in mid-air as just one edge of these sheets was resting on the ground. He committed two offences: one, never try jointing through more than one sheet of thin unpredictable material since it is likely to trap the blade as the sheet or sheets bend, causing a kickback. Two, never do this with the workpiece unsupported and uncramped because it is just floating and therefore uncontrollable. In his case, the damage to the ply was irrelevant since he needed eighteen stitches to his thigh.

Don't use your hand as a clamp. Another cabinetmaker I once knew tried holding a narrow moulding against a strip of wood fixed to the bench top and slotting it. His hand, acting as a clamp, was near the joiner, the blade of which struck a knot that flew out of its hole. It resulted in a trip to casualty and a wound on the tip of his finger that took a long time to heal.

Don't leave any power tools switched on at the wall sockets when you leave the workshop. Always err on the side of caution.

(KEY POINT

KEY POINT

The lesson with tool safety, especially power tools, is that accidents happen very fast but are usually predictable if you first analyse what you are about to do. Either the work or the machine *must* be firmly fixed.

Personal safety

Although we have covered several key points about using the biscuit joiner in the section on machine safety, there remains the question of how you protect yourself when woodworking.

Clothing

You must not wear sandals or open shoes as these invite injury to vulnerable feet from tools or wood being dropped, or just from stubbing your toe on the leg of a workbench. A good, tough pair of shoes or workboots, perhaps with steel toecaps are a good idea. Obviously you will need a set of workclothes that can get dusty or dirty; a woodworking apron is not vital these days, as most work is done with power tools and the front pocket will get full of chippings in no time. A turner's smock is quite good because it is enclosed at the front. Gloves are useful for handling large timber sections and boards – 'sticky' gloves are particularly good for this as they have thin lines of rubber which will grip on the board surfaces. Gloves also keep your hands warm in winter but can make hand operations difficult or impossible!

Dust

The biggest continuous hazard in the workshop is dust. In industry there are a lot of rules and regulations to prevent workers being exposed to dust hazards, but at home you have no such protection or knowledge of the real damage it can cause. For this reason I must insist that you take proper steps to protect yourself from the lethal effects of dust, especially the microfine dust particles which are invisible to the human eye. These are the particles that do serious damage to lungs, even if you don't do much woodworking, as the general dust produced can irritate eyes and lungs (and may even provoke an asthmatic attack should you happen to come into contact with an asthma sufferer after machining). At the very least, a simple preformed dustmask (sometimes called a monkey mask) will give a degree of protection; there are more sophisticated and expensive versions as well. A pair of protective work-glasses will give some protection against flying chippings (there shouldn't be much of this with a joiner, but err on the side of safety) although they won't stop sore itchy eyes. MDF (medium density fibreboard), which is much loved on TV room-makeover programmes, produces tons of fine dust particles when machined. If you do need to use it regularly, then a proper full-face powered respirator helmet such as the Racal Airlite is the only safe answer. This covers your face completely and a battery-powered motor draws air through a special filter designed to extract minute dust particles, leaving you with a stream of clean breathable air and no sore eyes. In theory even an asthma sufferer could do woodwork with one of these helmets if used correctly. There is a cost of course, but it makes long-term sense for good health.

Ear defence

Ears are very vulnerable to certain levels of noise and frequent machining can cause lasting damage which isn't readily apparent. A loss of sensitivity to sounds at certain frequencies, particularly softer sounds such as speech, and/or an onset of disturbing regular noises in the ears – a condition referred to as tinnitus – can spoil one's quality of life. There are ear defenders which fit over your head and cover the ears, but these are quite large and not necessarily comfortable. A lightweight solution is earplugs, which can be pushed gently into each ear. A slight drawback can be a tendency to push dirt or dust into the ears when putting them in. A newer type on the market can be washed and fitted in without suffering the drawbacks mentioned. Whatever type you choose, ear defence is a must.

In conclusion treat safety as a 'whole body' issue, not just a piecemeal thing to do when you can remember. Make it a habit.

ABOVE The Racal Airlite helmet is a very safe, cost-effective means of dust protection.

HELENA COLLEGE OF TECHNOLOGY LIBRARY
1115 NORTH ROBERTS
HELENA, MONTANA 59601

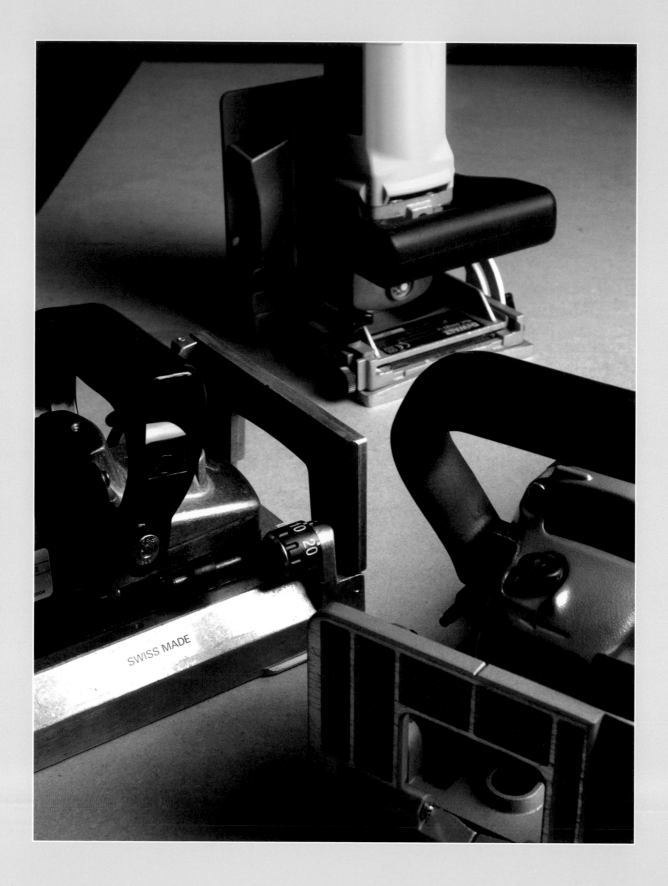

1:3 Biscuit joiner review

This is the chapter that should hopefully get any self-respecting joiner fanatic's fingers itching: a gallery of all the joiners I could get my hands on! In my experience, every joiner I have tried has performed pretty well, so it really comes down to price versus quality and personal likes and dislikes, such as the ergonomics of a particular model.

As you will see, there is a good choice of machines in differing price bands to suit all tastes and pockets. Most of us will be happy with one machine but anyone with the excuse might be tempted to buy two: for freehand and static setups; or one for jointing and one for sawing.

Choosing the right joiner

This gallery of models isn't exhaustive, especially as some machines are available under different brands and therefore aren't worth repeating. Really this is a chance for you to make a comparison of each model's specifications. Note that all these details were correct when this book went to press which means they probably aren't now! For that reason prices have not been included and it's best to check the woodworking press for up-to-date pricing.

Motor wattage is the input figure, not the output, as most manufacturers don't like to admit the efficiency (or inefficiency) of their motors. Depth settings are shown as 0, 10, 20, S, D and Max. The first three are the standard biscuit sizes; the next two are standard Lamello sizes for their specialist fittings; and the last is maximum cut depth, which can sometimes be tweaked using the fine adjuster to increase the depth of cut slightly.

It should be emphasized that all the joiners shown do their job but, as you might expect, the more expensive models can do more and with better accuracy of scales. If you are new to woodworking or biscuit jointing then a budget model may well suffice but in the long run a more advanced model may be a better investment.

Joiner gallery – Budget

Rexon 230v

• Voltage	240v
• Motor input	750w
• No load speed	10,000rpm
• Blade	4in (100mm) TCT
• Depth settings	0, 10, 20, S, D, Max
• Max. cut depth	$^{25}/_{32}$in (20mm)
• Fence adjustment	0–135°
• Weight	7.7lbs (3.5kg)
• Accessories supplied	Dustbag, wrench
• Special features	None

Ferm FBJ-710

• Voltage	240v
• Motor input	710w
• No load speed	11,000rpm
• Blade	4in (100mm) dia. TCT 6-tooth anti-kickback
• Depth settings	0, 10, 20
• Max. cut depth	$^5/_8$in (18mm)

- Fence adjustment   0–90°
- Weight   8.3lbs (3.8kg)
- Accessories supplied Dustbag
- Special features   Movable fence on slide slide rods

Draper PT8100A

- Voltage   230v
- Motor input   800w
- No load speed   11,000rpm

- Blade   4in (100mm) dia. 6-tooth TCT
- Depth settings   0, 10, 20
- Max. cut depth   0–$^{25}\!/_{32}$in (0–20mm)
- Fence adjustment   0–135°
- Weight   7lbs (3.2kg)
- Accessories supplied Dustbag, hex key
- Special features   None

Skil 1820 HJ

- Voltage   230–240v
- Motor input   710w
- No load speed   11,000rpm
- Blade   4in (100mm) dia. 4 tooth TCT
- Depth settings   0, 10, 20
- Max. cut depth $^{5}\!/_{8}$in (15mm)
- Fence adjustment   0, 45, 90°
- Weight   5.5lbs (2.5kg)
- Accessories supplied Blow mould case, dustbag, vacuum cleaner adaptor
- Special features   Fence is adjusted with two hex bolts instead of a lock lever

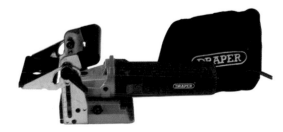

Joiner gallery – Budget

- Weight   7lbs (3.2kg)
- Accessories supplied   Blow mould case, dustbag, wrenches
- Special features   None

Clarke BJ600

- Voltage   230v
- Motor input   600w
- No load speed   11,000rpm
- Blade   4in (100mm) dia. TCT
- Depth settings   0, 10, 20, Max
- Max. cut depth   ⅝in (16mm)
- Fence adjustment   0–90°
- Weight   7lbs (3.2kg)
- Accessories supplied   Kit box, dustbag
- Special features   None

Axminster SLB9100N

- Voltage   240v
- Motor input   700w
- No load speed   10,000rpm
- Blade   4in (100mm) dia. TCT 6-tooth
- Depth Settings   0, 10, 20
- Max. cut depth   ⅞in (22mm)
- Fence adjustments   0–90°
- Weight   7lbs (3.2kg)
- Accessories supplied   Dustbag
- Special features   None

SIP Biscuit Joiner

- Voltage   240v
- Motor input   800w
- No load speed   11,500rpm
- Blade   4in (100mm) 6-tooth TCT anti-kickback
- Depth settings   0, 10, 20, Max
- Max. cut depth   ¾in (19mm)
- Fence adjustment   0–90°

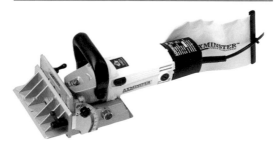

Joiner gallery – Mid-range

Makita 3901

- Voltage: 240v or 110v
- Motor input: 590w
- No load speed: 10,000rpm
- Blade: 4in (100mm) dia.
- Depth settings: 0, 10, 20, S, D, Max
- Max. cut depth: $^{25}/_{32}$in (20mm)
- Fence adjustment: 0–90°
- Weight: 6.1lbs (2.8kg)
- Accessories supplied: Blow mould case, dustbag, thickness plate, wrench
- Special features: Geared fence rise and fall, ribbed rubber anti-slip facing

Bosch GFF22A

- Voltage: 240v, 110v
- Motor input: 670w
- No load speed: 11,000rpm
- Blade: 4⅛in (105mm) dia. 8-tooth TCT anti-kickback
- Depth settings: 0, 10, 20, S, D, Max
- Max. cut depth: ⅞in (22mm)
- Fence adjustment: 0–90°
- Weight: 6.3lbs (2.9kg)

- Accessories supplied: Steel case, fence, dustbag two-hole wrench
- Special features: None

DeWalt DW682K

- Voltage: 240v, 110v
- Motor input: 600w
- No load speed: 10,000rpm
- Blade: 4in (100mm) dia. 6-tooth TCT anti-kickback
- Depth settings: 0, 10, 20, Max
- Max. cut depth: $^{25}/_{32}$in (20mm)
- Fence adjustment: 0–90°
- Weight: 6.6lbs (3kg)
- Accessories supplied: Heavy duty case, dustspout, shavings bag, wrench
- Special features: None

Joiner gallery – Mid-range

- Optional accessories   Pitch pocket cutter, Perspex baseplate, extraction hose
- Special features   None

Freud JS 102

- Voltage   240v
- Motor input   710w
- No load speed   10,000rpm
- Blade   4in (100mm) dia. TCT
- Depth settings   0, 10, 20, S, D, Max
- Max. cut depth $^{25}\!/_{32}$in (20mm)
- Fence adjustment   0–90°
- Weight   6.1lbs (2.8kg)
- Accessories supplied   Kit box, dustbag, blade wrench
- Special features   None

Lamello Classic C2

- Voltage   230v; 120v
- Motor input   705w
- No load speed   10,000rpm
- Blade   4in (100mm) dia. scribing 6-tooth TCT anti-kickback
- Depth settings   0, 10, 20, S, D, Max
- Max. cut depth $^{25}\!/_{32}$in (20mm)
- Fence adjustment   0–90°
- Weight   6.8lbs (3.1kg)
- Accessories supplied   Plastic kitbox, thickness plate, wrench, biscuits, two dustspouts
- Special features   None

Mafell LNF20; LN19

- Voltage   LNF20: 230v; LN19: 110v
- Motor input   750w
- No load speed   9800rpm
- Blade   4in (100mm) dia.
- Depth settings   0, 10, 20, S, D, Max
- Max. cut depth   ¾in (19mm)
- Fence adjustment   0–90°
- Weight   7lbs (3.2kg)
- Accessories supplied   Case, dustbag, dustspout

- Optional accessories 138in (3.5m) dust hose, repairing head CA64B, lateral fence CB64B
- Special features None

Lamello Experta

- Voltage 240v
- Motor input 705w
- No load speed 10,000rpm
- Blade 4in (100mm) dia. scribing 6-tooth TCT anti-kickback
- Depth settings 0, 10, 20, S, D, Max
- Max. cut depth 25/32in (20mm)
- Fence adjustments 0–90°
- Weight 6.8lbs (3.1kg)
- Accessories supplied None
- Special features None

Trend T20

- Voltage 240v
- Motor input 710w
- No load speed 10,000rpm
- Blade 4in (100mm) dia. TCT 6-tooth anti-kickback
- Depth settings 0, 10, 20, S, D, Max
- Max cut depth 25/32in (20mm)
- Fence adjustment 0–90°
- Weight 5.9lbs (2.7kg)
- Accessories supplied Blow mould case, dustbag, wrenches, oil
- Special features None

Virutex AB111N

- Voltage 230v
- Motor input 900w
- No load speed 10,000rpm
- Blade 4in (100mm) dia. 2-tooth and 2+2 spurs
- Depth settings 0, 10, 20
- Max. cut depth 25/32in (20mm)
- Fence adjustment 0–90°
- Weight 7lbs (3.2kg)
- Accessories supplied Carrying case, dustspout

Joiner gallery – Mid-range

Milwaukee PJ710

- Voltage — 240v
- Motor input — 710w
- No load speed — 10,000rpm
- Blade — 4in (100mm) dia. 6-tooth cutter (BG approved)
- Depth settings — 0,10, 20, S, D, Max
- Max. cut depth — ¾in (19mm)
- Fence adjustment — 0–90°
- Weight — 6.3lbs (2.9kg)
- Accessories supplied — Dustbag, dustspouts
- Special features — None

AEG LF650

- Voltage — 240v
- Motor input — 650w
- No load speed — 10,000rpm
- Blade — 4in (100mm) dia.
- Depth settings — 0, 10, 20, S, D, Max
- Max. cut depth — ¾in (19mm)
- Fence adjustment — 22.5°, 45°, 67.5°
- Weight — 6.3lbs (2.9kg)
- Accessories supplied — Dustbag, dustspouts,
- Special features — AEG CleanLine dustbag system, board thickness presetting

Joiner gallery – Professiona

DeWalt 685

- Voltage — 240v
- Motor input — 600w
- No load speed — 7500rpm
- Blade — 4in (100mm) dia. 12-tooth TCT anti-kickback
- Depth settings — ⅜–⅝in (10–18mm) adjustable
- Max. cut depth — 3¹⁄₃₂in (24mm)
- Fence adjustment — fixed 45° with attachment
- Min–max fence setting ⅜–2¾in (10–70mm)
- Weight — 6.1lbs (2.8kg)
- Accessories supplied — Metal case, dustspouts, dustbag, mitre joint attachment
- Optional accessories — 4⅛in (105mm) ply-cutting blade
- Special features — Swing-down body type

Lamello Top 20 S2

- Voltage   240v
- Motor input   500w (electronic speed control)
- No load speed   10,000rpm
- Blade   4in (100mm) dia. scribing TCT 6-tooth anti-kickback
- Depth settings   0, 10, 20, S, D, Max
- Max. cut depth $^{25}\!/_{32}$in (20mm)
- Fence adjustment   0–90°
- Weight   7.2lbs (3.3kg)
- Accessories supplied   Beechwood case, dustspouts, thickness plate
- Special features   Electronic speed control, 'Step Memory System' giving fine height adjustment of 0.1mm steps

Porter Cable 557

- Voltage   240v, 110v
- Motor input   750w
- No load speed   10,000rpm
- Blade   4in (100mm) dia. 6-tooth anti-kickback and 2in (50mm) dia. 4-tooth 'FF' blade.
- Depth settings   FF, 0, 10, 20, S, D, Max
- Max. cut depth $^{13}\!/_{16}$in (21mm)
- Fence adjustment   0–135°
- Weight   7.4lbs (3.4kg)
- Accessories supplied   Blow mould case, dustbag, thickness plate, 'FF' thickness plate, wrench
- Special features   Small 'FF'-size blade stage fence adjustment

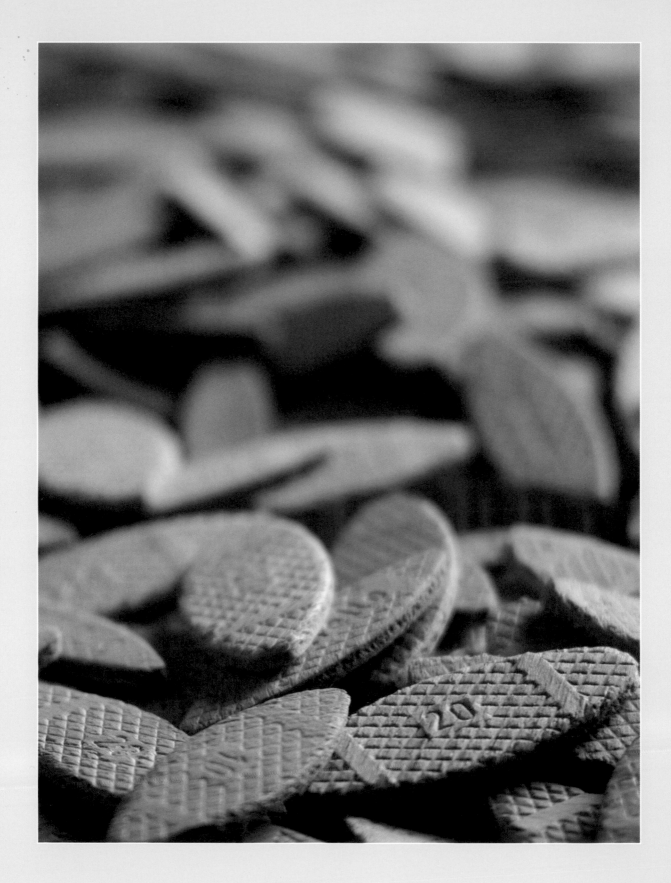

1:4 Consumables

In this chapter we will briefly cover a range of biscuit variants.
I still believe the standard beech biscuit is the best of the lot; the
more complex biscuit components are best left to professionals
with specific manufacturing needs. Any reader wanting to pursue
these more exotic options should get the latest up-to-date
information from the manufacturers or distributors concerned.

I have met a few woodworkers (only a few!) who begrudge the
cost of beech biscuits. I think they are so cheap and the resultant
joints so quick to produce that this point of view seems frankly
irrelevant. Choose a good quality brand of biscuits and glue, keep
the biscuits dry and the glue above freezing point, and you won't
go wrong. If biscuits are too tight for the slots, they may have
swollen with the damp or possibly the joiner blade may be badly
worn. Vernier callipers are ideal for checking biscuits, blades and
slots. Finally, always make sure you have plenty of biscuits in stock.

Beech biscuits

For 99% of all applications beech biscuits are just the ticket, but now and again we may have a need for a more unusual type of biscuit-based fitting. We will look at these later on but for now let's stick with our standard biscuit. I would suggest that when you first buy your joiner you buy a mixed pack of 500 or 1000 biscuits in the three standard sizes 0, 10 and 20. As you become more familiar with them I think you will find that 20s invariably get used much more than the smaller sizes, so when you restock, buy 1000 size 20s to reflect your general usage. When some time has passed you may need to restock the other sizes too, but 20s should remain the most important size unless you joint a lot of quite small components. Always use the biggest practical size because it will obviously hold the work together better. 0s in particular tend to break easily or have pieces missing whereas 20s and 10s have a bit more integrity. Always try to buy a proper branded make of biscuits as unbranded ones will be of uncertain origin and may prove to be of poor quality.

Ply biscuits

There are some beech ply biscuits on the market which, when produced correctly, have the advantage of not falling apart, as each ply holds the next one together with glue in between. As an option they are worth considering for their superior strength. My own experience is that they may be of variable thickness for whatever reason, possibly occurring when swollen by damp. Remember that biscuits will

ABOVE Size 0, 10 and 20 biscuits, and the smaller Lamello H9 (which needs a special cutter).

Transfer your biscuits into polythene ice-cream boxes, or similar food containers, or into sealed plastic bags (keeping the different sizes apart). That way you can prevent the biscuits swelling up when in storage.

RIGHT It is important not to let biscuits get damp and swell up in storage.

not fall apart once in the joint, it is only when they are sitting in the box waiting to be used that you may find some broken. Whatever type of biscuit you use, make sure you store them correctly.

Manufacturers normally supply them in corrugated cardboard boxes which doesn't keep moisture out but it does absorb some, thus helping to keep the biscuits dry.

ABOVE Solid wood (upper), ply (lower).

Technique

It's OK to gently tap biscuits into their slots with a hammer if you have a lot to fit or if they are a touch tight, but if this becomes a necessity then it means either the biscuits have swollen with damp or the joiner blade is quite worn. Since workshops are usually rather damp it is more likely to be the former. You can check your joiner blade's thickness using a vernier calliper on the blade or on the resulting slot.

ABOVE You can use a vernier calliper to check the size of your joiner blade.

When describing the joiner earlier on, I mentioned that there is a fine depth adjuster as well as multi-stage setting for biscuit sizes. After changing the fine setting for any reason make sure you reset it again and do some test slots to ensure they are not too deep or too shallow. You can push a biscuit into the slot and run a knife along the surface of the wood marking the side of the biscuit, turn the biscuit over and repeat. The gap or overlap between the knife lines is a good guide to resetting. The same depth requirement applies if you use a biscuit cutter with the router (this is preset by the bearing which is fitted). However, since the blade diameter is smaller than the joiner's and a lengthened slot is needed, there will be a gap at each end of the slot under the biscuit which will get filled with a lot of glue. This isn't ideal as the glue may take time to dry but you will just have to live with that.

ABOVE The slot cut by a biscuit joiner (right) is far more efficient than using a straight cutter in a router (left). A router-mounted biscuit cutter gives a reasonable slot shape (middle).

ABOVE A knife line will tell you whether the cut depth is correct.

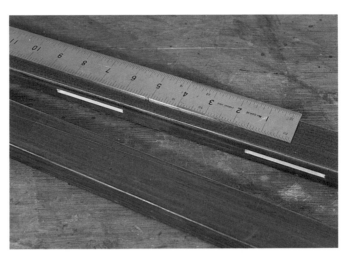

ABOVE Biscuit spacing is not critical but too close is a little wasteful and too much – more than say 10in (250mm) – loses strength.

You can place biscuits as close as you like but it makes economic sense to make the gapping 6–10in (150–250mm), 8in (200mm) being a good average. Although it can get a bit tedious and complex to do a dry assembly, it is a lot safer than assuming all your slots are OK and going straight ahead with gluing up. I'm guilty of doing this sometimes and mostly, because of my professional experience, I can get away with it. However, even I can get caught out and find a biscuit slot is misaligned or missing completely! At this point you have several components dripping with glue, some of which may have already gone together properly, and a desperate need to knock the whole thing apart in order to make things right. A sense of rising panic ensues when you realize that a simple error has become complex because you are in mid glue-up – hence the need to dry assemble, rather than assume that the ease with which you can slot a carcass will somehow see you through.

Occasionally it is even possible to accidentally miss something out, like a panel that slips into a groove. The carcass is fine, you've just forgotten the panel had to go in first! So what should you do in this unexpected situation? Firstly, don't panic – it isn't life threatening after all. Assess what steps you need to take to rectify matters. If a biscuit slot has been missed out, the carcass will probably go together OK, but if the biscuits are fitted in one joint half and you have one less slot in the other half, you will either need to make a emergency slot where it should have been or remove the biscuit in question. If other joints have to be taken apart you might have trouble because the biscuits may have swollen and the glue may have already started to bond. So with the carcass in this perilous and unstable state, we need to use a pair of pincers to

49

ABOVE Using pincers to remove a biscuit, a ⅛in chisel can clean out any remaining pieces of biscuit.

ABOVE Using a tenon saw to trim an errant biscuit off is a useful 'rescue' technique.

carefully tug the offending biscuit from its slot. It may break up and you will need a narrow chisel to prise the remains from the slot. An alternative is to use a small handsaw lying flat on the surface of the wood and gently trim the biscuit off flush with just a careful cut of a sharp chisel to ensure nothing is left projecting. The saw teeth may mark the surface but hopefully

this won't be too obvious once the carcass is properly assembled. One of the distinct advantages of beech is that it can be treated in this way as if it were any other piece of wood. If you do the unmentionable and make extra slots while there is glue already on the wood, remove all chippings so they don't get stuck to the wood and prevent the joint closing. Clean the joiner blade up and use a damp cloth to clean the sole and faceplate; also remove glue trapped in the dustspout as it will prevent chippings getting out – all this should be done with the power off of course!

It is easy to see all these biscuits and the accompanying glue just as pounds, shillings and pence but in fact they are an incredibly cheap, effective way to assemble anything in wood, so I personally don't have a problem with the cost of this very basic item.

Unusual wood biscuit sizes

It has taken a long time to happen, but gradually the beech biscuit has become a little more adventurous. Lamello currently produces smaller, thinner biscuits that suit equally small components and require a special thin blade, as well as super-size biscuits which require extended slots, rather like using a router for creating biscuit slots with its smaller diameter cutters. These extra large biscuits are also used in Lamello's special big industrial joiners which are normally used in sets operated by pistons, thus making mass production slotting possible. Lamello has more recently introduced a triple-decker biscuit and an extra long biscuit too. These types are ideal for furniture manufacturers but are of no great interest to the average user. Therefore the uses for these special biscuits are probably limited unless you have a particular purpose in mind, especially as they cost more than the standard type.

Triton, on the other hand, supplies biscuits designed for their biscuit-jointing accessory to the Series 2000 Workcentre, and these appeal to a lot of users. The biscuits are ³⁄₁₆in (4mm) thick, as usual, but are shorter and fatter as they have to fit into slots created by a router cutter. The unique feature of the Triton system is that having got a Workcentre, you then fit the optional router table and onto that the biscuit-jointing fence, thus giving a static setup. A router is installed with the special Triton biscuit cutter and the fence sits over the cutter. Then you mark your biscuit slots, adjust the stop on the fence and apply the component forming one half of the joint to the fence and push. The fence swings across, exposing the cutter which slots the wood; do the same with the matching component against the other side of the fence and your joint is cut. The result is precise, quick jointing using this swinging fence system and by adjusting the fence

ABOVE If you already own a Triton Workcentre the biscuit-jointing accessories are a sensible addition.

stop, all your slots can be cut in the same way. If you intend buying the Triton table anyway, for general sawing and routing, then this biscuit-jointing accessory makes a lot of sense as it gives precise static control. However, the biscuits, which only Triton produces, probably have limited use elsewhere (maybe someone reading this knows different!) and you will probably have to pay a bit more than for the standard type.

Porter Cable has created the tiny 'FF'-size biscuit which is a mere 1¼in (32mm) in length. They can be used for fine work or joining thin panels together. Thanks to the accuracy in the die-cutting of them, they seem to hold together better than the larger, standard size 0 biscuits. Porter Cable supplies a special small blade just for these biscuits – it normally comes as standard in the joiner kit.

FOCUS ON:

Glues and applicators

If you were to wet your biscuits under the tap they would swell up as if you were using a water-based glue and thus get trapped in the biscuit slots in the same way. However, you cannot rely on the swelling effect alone, as something more substantial is needed to complete the joint. Glues have been developed to a very high-tech level but the simplest and relatively cheap types work best. Since biscuits need water to swell up, water-based glues such as PVA are perfect. For most situations PVA will do for all your needs. It remains usable under most conditions except in winter as it gets very thick when cold. It dries fairly quickly too, providing it is used in reasonably warm conditions. In the trade it is usual to buy large, five-litre containers of glue, but as it needs to be decanted into smaller glue bottles or

applicators – which may be difficult as the glue is rather thick, even in warm conditions – it would be better to buy smaller amounts. A good quality PVA should be smooth and lump-free; do not allow it to freeze in a cold workshop or it will become weak and unusable. If you do buy in bulk, dispense some into small containers with nozzles for ease of application. Used washing-up liquid bottles are good for this, though you may need to cut out the star moulding under the nozzle to prevent it blocking up. You could use a Dosicol-type dispenser designed for biscuit slots; however, not only are they expensive, they are not meant for placing glue between slot positions and often deposit too much glue into each slot. The Minicol, with its point spout, or an ordinary glue bottle are fine. Complete glue dispenser

ABOVE The Lamello professional Dosicol glue dispenser, complete with waterbath unit to stop it clogging up.

ABOVE The Minicol is a cheaper unit, without the biscuit-shaped dispenser head.

ABOVE From left to right: PU glue (polyurethane), casein glue, aliphatic resin, PVA glue.

kits with a variety of nozzles are available, though these need to be kept clean and unblocked. For gluing large flat meeting faces, such as two boards to make up a thick desk top, a special glue applicator with a 'hopper' for the glue is ideal and worth the investment if you do this kind of work on a regular basis; Iin this case the biscuits don't need glue – they would just be there to aid location.

There are other glues, such as aliphatic resin glue which has a pale yellow colour and a sharp smell. It has a 'fast grab' which will make it difficult to use on a complicated glue-up as one part may start to set before you have cramped all of it up. It does remain runny during cold weather allowing it to remain usable in place of PVA, which thickens. Extramite powder glue is OK if mixed up rather runny, but is messy to

clear up and sometimes starts to set too quickly. It can also cause dermatitis, so disposable latex gloves or barrier cream are essential.

Another rather interesting glue is polyurethane. This needs moisture to activate it, when it starts to foam and expand. This is the recommended glue when using metal or plastic biscuit fittings as it swells to fill all the gaps and locks them in positively. You can accelerate the setting process by wiping one half of the joint face with a damp cloth. A means of holding the joint together is needed as the glue expands, unless the fittings have some kind of barb or ridge, which beech biscuits don't. If you need to use beech biscuits with polyurethane for some reason, lightly dampen the biscuits so they will swell up (a plant mist sprayer is good for this). Overall though, PVA glue is best.

ABOVE Lamello assembly biscuits have ridges to lock components together.

Assembly biscuits

For 'try outs' and awkward assembly situations there are special assembly biscuits available from Lamello. These are bright red plastic and have ridges or barbs making non-cramp assembly theoretically possible. Other manufacturers, such as Knapp, produce biscuits with similar features; they aren't one piece like Lamello's but demountable two-part biscuits which are proper joint-forming biscuits. I have my doubts as to whether assembly biscuits designed to be fully removable are really useful as they damage the sides of the slots when pulled out. However, as a means of attaching parts such as mouldings, permanently and invisibly, they are very useful especially on site where no adequate means of cramping is available. I believe that without exception, all specialist biscuit type fittings, including assembly biscuits, can be glued in place if needed. Usually polyurethane glue is the preferred type as it expands to fill all gaps and the excess can be cleaned off easily once dry.

Specialist consumables

Lamello might have started the whole biscuit thing but there are other manufacturers beavering away to design and produce their own high-tech fixing solutions that take advantage of the humble biscuit slot. Here are some of the more exotic items you can buy, providing you don't mind spending the money!

Lamello

Strangely Lamello hasn't devoted quite as much effort to metal or plastic biscuit fixings as some of their competitors. Nevertheless certain items, such as the

ABOVE Lamello consumables: left side top to bottom: demountable hinge, Corian plate, detachable fitting, assembly biscuit; right side top to bottom: comparison with standard size 20, 10 and 0 biscuits.

cabinet hinge fittings, are unique and add an interesting touch to a good quality piece of furniture. They are available both in the UK and the US, as well as in Europe.

Knapp

German brand Knapp has come up with a wide range of biscuit fittings for all kinds of uses. A key feature is that they are all demountable, being two-part clip or slide together fittings. They sell their own special polyurethane assembly glue as well.

Hafele

This is another large European furniture trade supplier, with a headquarters in the UK. Biscuit fittings are a minor part of their vast catalogue but as far as I know these fittings are unique to them. This push-together type with the rubber band around them are meant for one-time assembly only. Hafele is also available throughout the US.

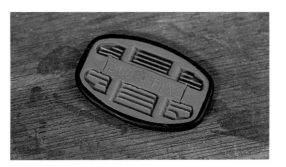

ABOVE Hafele supplies many types of non-biscuit fastenings but this one-way barbed device with a rubber retaining band is an interesting one.

Lamifix

This is a small Swiss company started by the owner of a joinery company. These fittings aren't sold in the UK and have limited distribution on the Continent but are an interesting system of fixings. The use of steel plates with screw threads grafted on make them quite different, as do the small holes through the plates for fixing screws. Availability is confined to Europe although they would probably supply elsewhere on request.

ABOVE Some unusual biscuit fastenings for different situations, mostly demountable.

ABOVE From a relatively small Swiss manufacturer, the Lamifix fastenings are all-metal and cover a variety of furniture assembly situations.

Part 2:
Techniques

2:1 Planning joints and marking out

All woodworking disciplines entail planning and marking out and the biscuit joiner is no different. Joiner users often come unstuck by not planning and marking out properly. A notepad, pencil and calculator, plus a steel rule, are essential for getting a good result. Define what you are trying to do and where it will be used and how. Then work out the overall size and any special requirements. From this you can then do a drawing (a sketch will often do) and from this drawing start to formulate a list of components. Remember to add or subtract the thickness of adjoining material as necessary because one piece usually has to fit inside or against another piece. Do not rely on mental arithmetic – a calculator is much more exact than the average human brain. Group components on paper where they are the same size and check how economically you can cut them out of a standard sheet of board material. Always remember fence-to-blade offset distances when using the joiner to saw out. Use simple aids, such as an index stick for accurate repetition marking and getting components the right way round. Practice, as they say, makes perfect – well almost.

ABOVE Careful setting out and accurate jointing has ensured this carcass has gone together correctly.

Planning joints

Except for very simple jointing situations the planning of the assembly order and the correct marking out are essential for success. Take a storage unit with shelves for example. This would end up as a disaster if care and thought weren't exercised at the planning stage. Firstly, the parts need to be accurately cut (see chapter 2:5) and then the relationship of each joint must be understood. Placing all the unjointed parts in their correct positions and lightly cramping them allows careful marking of each joint to be done. As we have previously seen, a degree of tolerance is possible because each joint has some lateral movement once assembled. Nevertheless, for the best result it is good practice to mark across each joint position with the components accurately aligned. Where T-joints are needed, such as for shelves in the bookcase, you need to use a decently large marking square to draw across the board where each shelf will go and, of course, mark clearly whether the shelf goes above or below each line, to avoid mishap.

When machining slots in board edges make sure you get the board the right way up in relation to the joiner. In other words, if you mark the joint on one face, the joiner fence will sit on that face as it is the 'reference' face of the machine as well as the workpiece.

ABOVE When marking up T-joints and carcasses it helps to place the parts together first to get accurate positioning.

ABOVE The shelf position is marked, the arrow showing the shelf will go underneath the line.

If you do the same operation with the joiner sitting on a reference board *without* using the fence, the workpiece is inverted and the reference face of the workpiece is underneath because this time, the underside of the joiner acts as the reference face of the machine. This has implications because the fence can, with care, be set at any position so the slot is where you want it, but when using a reference board, the slot position is determined by the distance of the joiner base to the blade which is fixed – unless you use packers (see chapter 2:3 for more). Not surprisingly, this kind of mental juggling makes a lot of woodworkers opt for the freehand method whenever

ABOVE Using the fence for freehand jointing.

ABOVE The joiner is sitting on a reference surface with the fence holding the workpiece down.

ABOVE An index stick speeds up marking out and ensures identical slot positions.

possible but as we shall soon see, this isn't always a good move and may not always be possible.

Sometimes a lot of components have joint positions that are effectively the same from piece to piece. Now, although it isn't good to swap components around at assembly time, and each component should be properly marked to show its position in the carcass, it is possible to make up a simple indexing stick with the correct number of 'strike marks' on it. This can then be used to quickly mark all similar joints with repeatable accuracy, which saves time and headaches.

Mistakes do happen, so check all slots have been properly cut. If one is slightly out of line you can either glue a biscuit in the slot, saw off the projecting part when dry and attempt a new slot in more or less the same position – though this may not be successful because of the degree of overlap – or you can make a new pair of slots in a new position, if that is possible. You can dry assemble with some, rather than all the biscuits to see how the piece is going together; a pair of pincers are useful

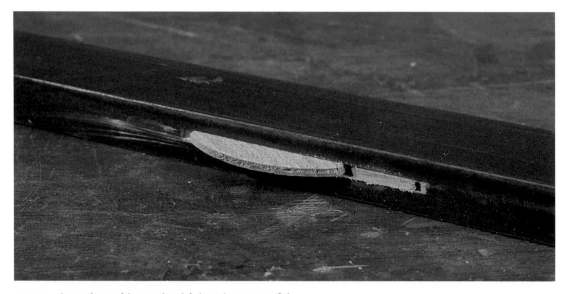

ABOVE Sometimes this repair trick is quite successful.

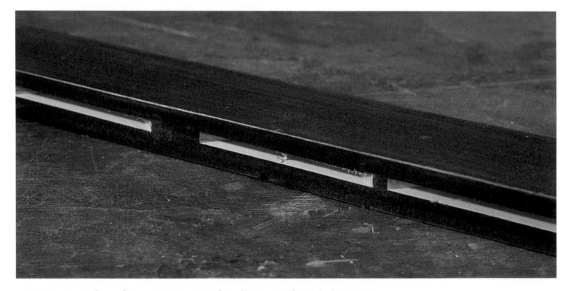

ABOVE It may be safer to create new slots between the existing ones.

for removing these easily once the assembly has been checked. Very narrow components can be slotted on the end but the strike marks need to be centred so the biscuit slot (which is longer than the biscuit itself) does not 'break out' at one side (this is best done in a static setup – see chapter 2:8).

The actual spacing between biscuits isn't critical and too many can be wasteful – general recommendations seem to suggest that 6–10in (150–250mm) spacing is OK. Narrow components, say 5in (120mm) wide, need two size 20 biscuits close together for proper strength. You end up with something rather like a semi continuous tongue-and-groove joint.

To sum up: mark accurately, cut accurately and machine accurately, and if any of these stages don't quite work out right, don't give up, use a bit of ingenuity to put it right – the joiner allows you to do this!

ABOVE Extracting a biscuit the easy way.

ABOVE Two biscuits in the end of a narrow board give plenty of strength and flush surfaces.

KEY POINT

Where a component gets missed out or a later addition is needed, then it may be possible to mark and fit this part later by slotting the offending item and sliding it onto biscuits fixed in the carcass (see chapter 2:6).

KEY POINT

Freehand

The basics of using the joiner have been covered in chapter 1:2. However, there are various ways of using and getting the best from your machine. Not all joiners handle the same way although the design may be similar. As an example the Lamello models have slightly cramped handgrips and the rear of the body is on the large side, while the DeWalt plunge model has a larger, squarer handgrip and a very small rear body end with the switch trigger integrated into it. These sorts of differences mean that a slightly different working method or way of holding may be developed as a result of using them.

In the case of the DeWalt 'straight-ahead' model, it is unwise to pick it up or hold it by the rear trigger as it will instantly start the motor running. When working in cramped areas the handgrip may need to be unbolted or swung down onto the body where possible, but some models may not be able to do this, which could influence your choice of machine if you do a lot of site work or installations.

The most obvious way to hold a joiner is to use a combination of handgrip and the rear of the body, though you can sometimes hold the top of the blade housing front face once the machine is sitting on the workpiece. This assumes

ABOVE An ergonomic comparison of Porter Cable and Stayer machines.

ABOVE Working stance: holding the loop handle.

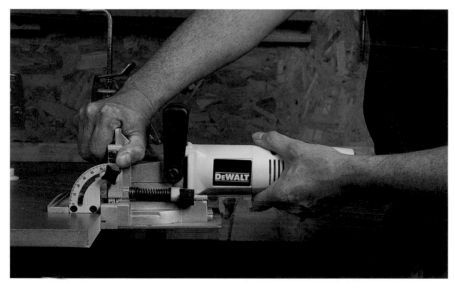

ABOVE Working stance: holding the front plate.

that you have cramped the workpiece and are operating freehand. If you are trying to joint into narrow edges this may not be very satisfactory for several reasons. Firstly, it can be difficult to offer the machine dead square onto such a narrow surface ready to cut, especially as you cannot observe the position of the fence and body face vis-à-vis the workpiece from the side, so a little practice at rocking the joiner slightly and pressing it into position until it feels right is useful, but without actually plunging.

The sprung pins or rubber pads used to prevent the machine slipping sideways may not help in judging how square the joiner is to the wood as these devices project slightly from the blade housing faceplate. Also some joiners are made with a slight recess in the fence where it meets the joiner's front face; and some fences have slightly raised surfaces which do not match the frame that holds them. Therefore the workpiece, if say ¾in (20mm) or less in thickness, may slip into this resulting recess causing the slot to be a fraction lower down the board face (when working from the face side, not the edge) and thus a corner joint where a face and edge meet will not align properly.

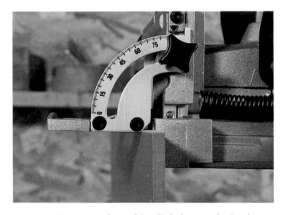

ABOVE A narrow board is slightly caught in the fence recess, and therefore the biscuit position will be wrong.

Another vital point is that the material you are using must have adjacent faces at 90° to each other; straightness of faces and edges *will* affect the overall result, though not necessarily each individual biscuit joint. So, for narrower work it may be better to sit both the joiner and workpiece on a flat surface (see next section).

Wider workpieces can be jointed freehand more successfully because they contact with more of the fence or front face of the joiner with greater accuracy. When biscuit jointing smallish moulding sections onto a carcass it is tempting to try and slot the mouldings freehand but this can end in disaster (see chapter 1:2) so a safe static setup is needed (see chapter 2:8). At the other end of the scale it is just about possible to machine slots right along an 8ft (2.4m) piece of board, either as a strip or full board width with only support in the middle, but it isn't wise.

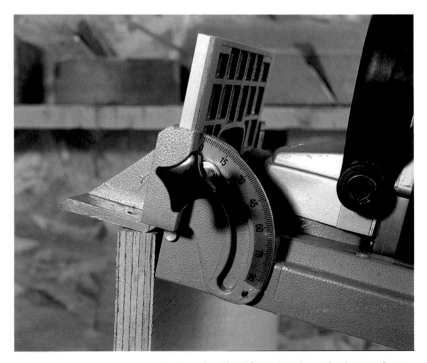

ABOVE The tilted faceplate is pushed away from work, resulting in an inaccurate slot.

Apart from the board flapping about in the wind and causing inaccurate joints, it may be hazardous too. Always use proper work supports and in the case of narrow but long strips of board it is worth making up the joiner working table (see project 3:5) whose length and strong box section make jointing awkward workpieces much easier. Having said all that it is possible to work freehand very quickly if you are confident that all your joint marking is correct. A carcass or a succession of parts can be dealt with at a speed no other machine can match, though you need to keep an eye on the standard of accuracy with such repetitious working.

RIGHT Joiner table (project 3:5).

KEY POINT

When using known board thicknesses on a regular basis, cut small blocks of scrap material after slotting in exactly the correct position, whether that means centred or off-centred in the thickness of the board. Mark the upper faces (the ones that will be against the fence) of these 'thickness blocks' and keep them handy for quickly adjusting the fence setting each time. When you need to use one, turn off the machine, push the block onto the plunged blade and slide the fence up to the block and lock it. Quick, easy setting for repeat working!

ABOVE A set of thickness blocks allows rapid resetting of the joiner fence for standard board thicknesses.

KEY POINT

Working on a flat reference surface

This effectively means using a static setup: a good flat board that you can rely on. Melamine-faced chipboard is not suitable as it can bend easily and the shiny facing

ABOVE The joiner sitting on a reference board while slotting an edge.

ABOVE In order to offset the slot position, the joiner is sitting on a packer.

doesn't stop the machine slipping around. Ideally a ¾in (19mm)+ thick piece of MDF, ply or blockboard, with a smoothish surface is best. This in turn should be lying on a flat bench top or similar so that it cannot bow and cause any slot misalignment.

The reason for working on a flat board is that the face and baseplate of the biscuit joiner blade housing have been machined true to the blade and at 90° to each other, thus giving greater accuracy than using the fence and freehand method when slotting board edges. It may be necessary to pack the joiner or the workpiece where one is raised in relation to the other, so that the slot is correctly aligned in the board edge. This doesn't mean centred, because you may need the slot offset for some good reason. A selection of thin packing pieces, such as Formica offcuts or very thin ply or hardboard, allow suitable adjustment though this mustn't allow either the machine or the workpiece to 'float' on the packers – a little downward pressure may be needed to ensure accuracy or it may be better to glue or pin the packers in position. With this method always cramp the workpiece down anyway, because with any hand or machine operation either the tool or the wood must stay fixed; in this case, the wood. Some machines come with a special clip-on 'thickness plate' which serves a similar purpose but is attached to the fence, thus being intended for freehand working. The joiner fence can be pushed down and locked, which will act as a 'hold-down' to keep the workpiece flat so long as it is carefully set.

☾KEY POINT

To slot the face of a workpiece with the joiner sitting on a board requires a simple jig; otherwise the board will be vertical and unsupported or the joiner may be upright, in which case it needs a high wooden fence to press against (see chapter 2:8).

ABOVE Many joiners come with a thickness plate for easy adjustment of the slot position in a board edge.

☾KEY POINT

ABOVE Joiner fence set to hold the work down.

2:2 Sanding, gluing, cramping and cleaning up

It is no good planning, marking, cutting and jointing if the right steps in preparing the timber or board are not taken or if proper assembly technique is not observed. Timber needs to be planed and properly flat and true; pre-assembly sanding is common sense but most of us don't do it properly and then it is impossible to put right after glue-up. Gluing technique is crucial: too much or too little glue, perhaps in the wrong place, could cause problems cleaning up the mess or joints starved of glue precipitating early failure. Fortunately the nature of the biscuit joint and the hydraulic pressure that is applied to the glue on joint closure helps prevent weak joints but exuding messy glue is another matter.

It is worth investing in a decent number of cramps of which there are various types on the market. Smaller 'G' or 'F' cramps are useful but so too are sash or board cramps, especially as the joiner is ideally suited to carcass work (furniture). There are quite a lot of cheap imported cramps which offer better value for money when buying a few. Luckily the expansive nature of the biscuit allows us to move cramps along to new positions once the first ones have swollen and the joints are holding together tightly. The biscuit is a very benign joining device if we use it sensibly.

Preparation

Firstly, all intended internal carcass surfaces and other hard-to-reach areas must be sanded to a finish before assembly, while exterior surfaces should be sanded to an adequate degree so that most of the work is done before the whole thing goes together. If sanding is left until later it becomes harder to do and doesn't look or feel very nice because the resultant finish will be so rough. Flat surfaces and mouldings are much more easily sanded individually.

FOCUS ON:

Sanding

FOCUS ON:

Sanding

My own recipe for success is to start with a belt sander (with a sanding frame if available), using 80 grit then 120 grit belts (new, sharp 120 grit only, if sanding veneered boards). This must be done with the grain as cross-grain scratches are impossible to remove. Then use a small random orbital sander and velcro-fixed abrasive discs in 180, 220 and 320 grit types (120 grit is OK for coarser joinery work). Note that I said 'random' orbital – the standard orbital sanders that most woodworkers use give a poorer finish and can be painfully slow. Nowadays there

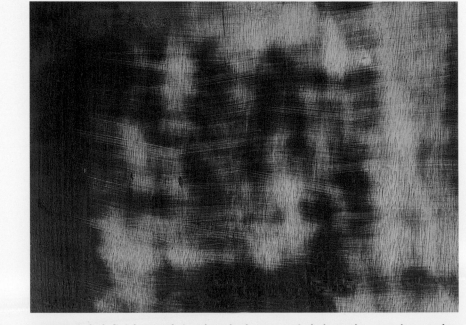

ABOVE A dark finish reveals just how bad cross-grain belt sander scratches can be.

Assembly technique

Especially with more complicated pieces you need to be organized and work out the correct assembly order or whether it is possible to make up several sub-assemblies first, before bringing these together once the glue is dry. Lock the workshop door and ignore the phone; get help if the work is awkward to do on your own – you need to concentrate just on the job and nothing else.

is a wide range of random orbitals, including some fairly cheap ones. These are quick and very efficient at removing their own sanding marks as they go, which means coarser abrasives can be used if necessary. The velcro feature makes quick changes from one grit to another. Where hand sanding is needed, use at least 150 grit aluminium oxide paper and preferably 220, 240 or 320 to give a fine finish. Hand sanding should really only need to be done on mouldings and edges; good machine sanding gives a much better finish.

ABOVE A professional random orbital sander and abrasives.

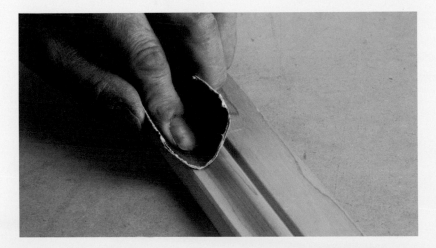

LEFT Hand sanding should be left for mouldings and other awkwardly shaped components.

Gluing up

Gluing technique is important: too little means a joint can fail but too much just makes a mess to be cleaned up. The best thing is to run a thin line of glue along one edge so it trickles into the biscuit slots, then apply glue to the slots only on the other joint half. Push the biscuits into this

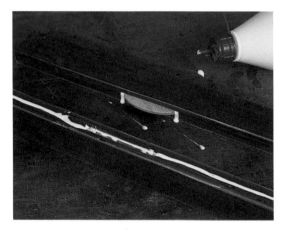

ABOVE A typical glue application with glue only in the slots on one half.

second lot of slots, which will help hold the glue in while you lift it over the other half to assemble the joint; then close the joint, ensure the strike marks line up and that edges and ends also align properly.

I believe it is important to have glue between biscuits but not too much, hence the technique described above. Solid wood in particular will benefit from the extra glue as the long grain will naturally bond giving extra strength. Components with a gluing surface wider than 1in (25mm) need a zig-zag pattern of glue laid down and the larger the area, the bigger the zig-zag pattern. For instance, with a desk top made from two boards face to face, it isn't necessary to apply glue to every single square inch of surface; a good even pattern over the whole area will do the job and once any pressure is applied to the joint it will begin to spread.

ABOVE A wide zig-zag glue pattern is best for larger components.

Cramping and cleaning up

Have plenty of cramps of suitable sizes for
the job in hand and apply these carefully,
using pads to prevent marking the work,
so that pressure is put on the joints without
distorting the carcass or pushing it out
of square. If necessary move the cramp
positions until everything is OK. Use a
square (preferably an engineer's square) to
check all the corners and use a steel tape
rule for diagonal corner-to-corner checking,
ensuring that the measurements agree and
the carcass is truly square. All this should be
done on a flat surface to prevent distortion.
You only need cramps on alternate biscuit
positions, which should be moved after a
while to ensure the other biscuit joints also
close properly. The first ones should be
OK because the biscuits will have already
swollen, thus locking the joints closed.

Once you are satisfied, the glue can be
removed with a 'second best' chisel and
a damp cloth, though it may be easier
to leave until it has gone plasticky and
started to set; it can then be cleaned off
with a chisel, which avoids getting water
on the work (which raises the grain and
the wood then needs resanding). Once
the glue has dried, check all is well and
do any minor work such as drilling or
trimming any projecting parts. Then give
the outside a fine sanding and lightly
hand sand all edges to remove any
sharpness to the touch.

ABOVE Good cramping technique
will ensure a carcass stays square.

ABOVE The cramps need to be
moved outwards slightly to prevent
the carcass sides bowing in.

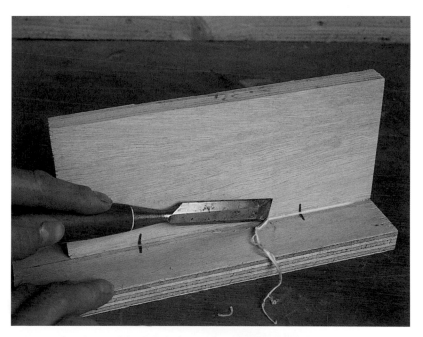

ABOVE Cleaning up 'plasticky' glue with a chisel.

2:3 Different ways of using the biscuit

The humble beech biscuit may seem limited in application but as this chapter shows there are quite a few jointing variations we can use. Ally it to different biscuit sizes to suit different material thickness and we have an excellent all-round jointing system.

Sometimes the biscuit may be no more a locational aid – when doubling material thickness for an office desktop for example – but the ease and convenience of ensuring exact component alignment, when wet glue can easily cause displacement, marks the biscuit out as an exceptional assembly aid. The more you work with a biscuit joiner the more you discover its limits of accuracy and what it is capable of. Eventually, setting out offset joints and T-joints becomes second nature and you wonder how you managed before. Problematic picture frame joints become a cinch, especially with a static setup (chapter 2:8) and picture frame clamps. No matter what you want to do with a biscuit there is invariably an answer.

If we stick with the standard three biscuit sizes 0, 10 and 20, there are various ways of using them which extend their basic function and therefore that of the joiner too, allowing it to do more kinds of work than might at first appear (for a detailed look at using biscuits see chapter 1:4). Let's go through each joint in turn.

Edge-to-edge joint

This is very easy to achieve, either freehand or on a reference board. The two reasons for using it are to increase the width of a board or to put different materials together, i.e. solid wood and veneered board.

Increasing board width

In the first example it might be to increase a board beyond its existing size, such as for a bookcase back panel which is wider than a standard 4ft (1.2m) board width; perhaps to make more economical use of offcuts;

or possibly to correct a mistake! Veneered board can be particularly successful done this way so long as the joint is done along and not across the grain, and the pattern and colour of the grain is well matched. It is certainly possible to slot MDF board that is just ¼in (6mm) thick, provided that the blade is very accurately centred on the board edge and the board has proper support along the edge when plunging. Biscuits should be close together too, as thin board will flex, making a less than

ABOVE The edge-to-edge joint is the most basic joint.

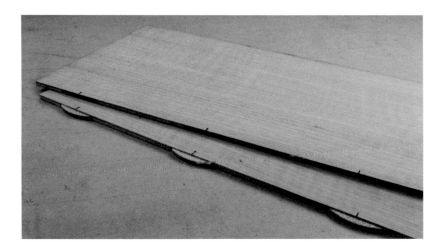

LEFT If the slots are perfectly centred on thin board, edge-to-edge joints can work very well.

flush joint along its length. Care is needed when sanding all veneered board as slight surface differences do occur and it is easy to 'rub through' the facing veneer. Also be aware that thin board will puff slightly at each joint and distortion of the surface at each joint may show up when a finish is applied to the wood. Incidentally you can mock up a table top, complete with mitred frame effect or 'breadboard ends' by jointing strips of the same veneered board around the edge of the centre panel.

When used to joint solid wood boards to make door panels which are 'raised and fielded', i.e. with the panel edges machined down for a 'raised panel' effect, take care with biscuit positions. It is very easy to have biscuits in their slots 'grinning' through, where the panel cutter has sliced straight through the middle of a biscuit. The answer is to plan the joint positions according to how the panel will be trimmed to size and what amount the panel cutter will take away – forethought, in other words!

Jointing different materials

This is useful if you want, for instance, a centre panel of man-made board with a solid wood frame for strength and appearance. There is no difference in technique, though the timber may be a bit tougher to machine than the board if the blade is starting to go blunt. If you want the panel recessed (set back) then

obviously the fence will need to be set further from the blade when slotting the frame. Apart from doing a test piece to check the result, this isn't any more difficult than a flush joint.

ABOVE We've all done it – a biscuit showing on the edge of a raised panel. This is avoidable with a little forethought.

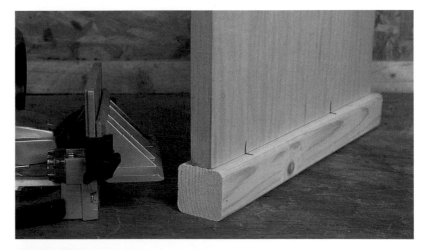

ABOVE Being able to join components of different thicknesses is extremely useful.

Corner joint

This is the cornerstone, you might say, of carcass building since most furniture carcasses have four corners. Providing your joiner fence will sit accurately on a narrow edge for doing the face cut, there is no reason why you shouldn't do this joint freehand. If there is any doubt or you would like more control, then a simple L-jig setup (see chapter 2.8) will make the face slotting easy, while the edge slotting can be done flat down on your reference board. As always, remember to mark the biscuit positions on the outside faces but transfer them to the inside faces, as these are the ones that you will see when machining. Use an index stick to simplify the marking out.

ABOVE Transferring biscuit marks to the other face allows accurate biscuit slotting on a reference board.

ABOVE The corner joint is probably the most used biscuit joint.

T-joint

This is the joint that can fox woodworkers completely; some may have never heard of it! This is a shame really, because once you get the hang of it, it allows more complex carcass work and much easier fitting of offset components. Suppose you have two sides of a bookcase, as before: you know the spaces needed for the books and you know the thickness and number of shelves. So mark all shelf positions on one bookcase side showing the shelf locations clearly and transfer these positions accurately to the other half by lying them side by side. Now nominate either the top or the bottom face of the shelves as the reference for the joiner base. With any luck, the joiner blade position, if not in the middle of each shelf, will at least not be too far off it. This allows us to do the shelf end slots on our reference board without

packers. The bookcase side slots can be done by cramping a T-square (see project 3:3) along each reference line in turn and pressing the joiner against it for accurate fencing. If your joiner has some form of anti-slip device then you can simply sight down the base of the joiner carefully and plunge slowly, without using a fence at all (see chapter 1:2). This isn't as bad as it sounds, in fact I do it as a matter of course.

ABOVE The T-square is a must for doing shelf slots like these.

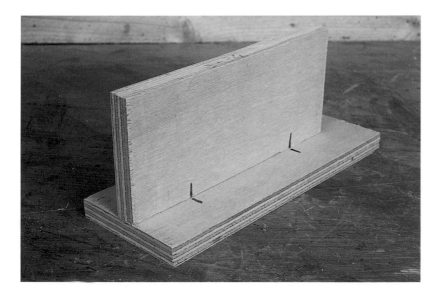

LEFT T-jointing is vital for many projects.

ABOVE If you have a firm hand and a good eye, T-jointing without a fence is perfectly possible.

ABOVE Making a thicker workpiece from two boards couldn't be simpler.

Do hold the loop handle though to avoid kickback; if the slots are slightly misaligned the shelf should still go onto the biscuits OK. The T-joint allows all kinds of parts to be assembled well away from the joiner's own fencing limit which is normally close to the board's edge, and is therefore an invaluable part of the biscuit joiner's repertoire. The router used for jointing cannot do this, though a ³⁄₁₆in (4mm)-wide straight cutter will produce a usable slot, albeit the wrong shape which will get filled with an excessive amount of glue. See chapter 2:4.

Face-to-face joint

This may not seem to be particularly necessary, but in fact face-to-face work broadens the scope of the joiner yet again. Two good reasons are: to increase the thickness of stock that you're able to work with; and to prevent components slipping around when glued-up during cramping. With this method always fence off one face only, because if you try working off opposing faces the slots won't all line up – try and prove me wrong!

If your machine has a high front plate it may be possible to get two rows of biscuits a reasonable distance apart. Using this method you could for instance knock up 4in x 4in (100mm x 100mm) newel posts for a staircase using standard 4in x 2in (100mm x 50mm) softwood doubled up.

It also allows the use of well-seasoned hardwood, where hardwood twice the thickness may not be well seasoned or stable enough to use. It is important to note, as with all jointing work, that good joints start with well-prepared surfaces and access to a planer/thicknesser will ensure good meeting surfaces when using hardwoods. Softwoods tend to be fairly well produced in their prepared state but check with an accurate try-square before using. Arising from the need to double material thickness is the problem of how to stop the two pieces slipping around when glued-up and the cramps applied. As glue is slippery, viscous stuff, it is very difficult to get the component edges flush. If you were going to biscuit them anyway, the problem of 'slip' solves itself. If, however, you didn't feel biscuits were necessary, the answer is still to use a few biscuits just to positively locate both pieces. An example suggested earlier was that of a large desk top formed from two sheets of veneered MDF; because of its size, biscuiting all over isn't possible but location biscuits ensure that one edge is flush and you can then tap the end of one sheet with a block and mallet so that the ends line up too. Lastly, it must be placed on a flat surface, with plenty of heavy weights applied all over to hold both sheets together until the glue has dried.

ABOVE Tapping two boards flush after glue-up; the strike marks make alignment easy.

Boxed-up joints

The boxed-up joint is nothing more than four corner joints all close together to form a very rigid hollow square shape. This is ideal for table legs, for example, and is immensely strong. As always the components need to be carefully cut to start with, but providing the edges are a true 90° to the faces, once glued and the cramps are put on, the box shape will pull together very straight and square, and once dry is almost indestructible. The ends don't particularly need to be plugged or capped but this is an option if you can cut pieces accurately enough to fit. If this joint is done in solid wood the resulting joints aren't very noticeable; however, plain MDF, or veneered boards which need the edges taped with veneer may be a bit more obvious. One way round this is to use the joiner in shallow 'saw mode' and run a groove down each joint and on the unjointed faces as well, to give a deliberate decorative effect that disguises the joints (see chapter 2:7).

ABOVE The boxed-up joint is strong and almost indestructible.

Mitres

Most of the time cabinet work consists of square joints, but every now and then mitred joints are needed. Mouldings such as cornices and plinths need neatly mitred junctions and sometimes a design may call for an angled shape – a corner cupboard that literally fits across the corner of a room for example.

All joiners can slot 45° mitres using the fence, which can normally be reversed so the 45° face comes into play. More sophisticated models have been equipped so that the fence can swing right down to give variable mitre angles including acute ones (as in the case of the Draper or the Flex Porter Cable) or the actual front plate on the blade housing may swing down parallel to the blade (Lamello Top Twenty, Classic, etc) which, although not as extreme as the former examples, is still very useful. In all cases the work has to be clamped down and the machine brought to the work rather than the other way round. A certain amount of care is needed in order to be successful. Machining into narrow, end-grain mitres must be done with the sprung spikes or other anti-slip devices in place because there is more likelihood of a kickback, where the machine will move suddenly to one side thus damaging the slot and perhaps hazarding the operator.

ABOVE Obtuse angle mitring showing the gap caused by the anti-slip devices.

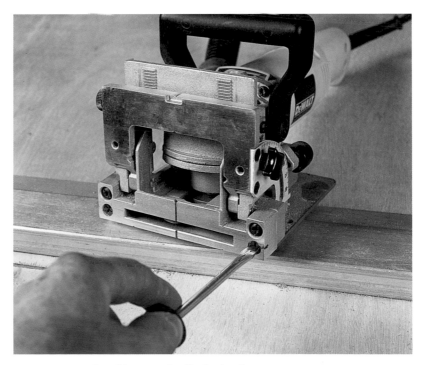

ABOVE Retracting this type of spike is simple – there is a screwdriver slot for the purpose.

KEY POINT

KEY POINT

No matter how you machine a mitre slot, it is vital that you plunge slowly to avoid any kickback and to get accurate positioning of the slot, although the wood may burn, especially as end grain is tougher, with a consequent blackening of the blade. These burnt deposits should be cleaned off or this will only get worse with all subsequent biscuit slotting.

ABOVE A useful kit of blade-cleaning and honing gear.

Unfortunately these anti-slip devices tend to prevent the joiner from seating onto the mitre face properly. This is particularly true with the standard mitre fence which only allows an obtuse angle between the fence and the front face of the joiner. Those machines that have full swing-down fences can 'trap' the mitre because the angle between the fence and front face is an acute one, usually at 45°. Here the need for anti-slip devices is less and they are worth avoiding, so the machine can sit tightly in the correct location.

Mitres must be cut accurately to work well. A radial arm saw or chopsaw with a fine

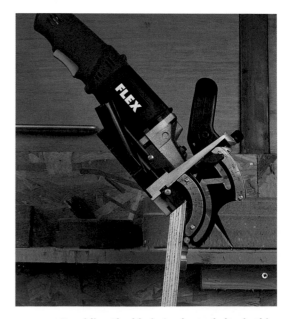

ABOVE Providing the blade is plunged slowly this kind of 'trapped mitre' is safe and accurate.

blade is needed to get good results and plenty of test pieces should be cut to check that all the mitres are true and will meet nicely. It isn't a good idea to try mitring on long edges, such as when making a boxed-up shape. This is because it is difficult to get four (or more) long edge mitres that meet well without some truly accurate means of machining them.

Flat mitres, such as for picture or mirror frames, are natural for the joiner. If the frame width is narrow, however, the biscuit slots and the biscuits may show at either side. It is possible to offset the biscuit slightly to the inside edge where there will be rebate for the picture or mirror anyway and the biscuit can just be trimmed off. All flat mitre joints tend to be a bit weak so if the wood is thick enough, you may be able to use two biscuits, one above the other. Since some joiners have a gap in the middle of the fence and because you will be cutting into narrow end grain which may cause a kickback, the rule is to use a static setup for safety and accuracy. This is easy to do and uses the flat underside of the frame as the reference face (see chapter 2:8).

ABOVE By choosing the right biscuit size it is possible to hide the jointing method completely.

2:4 Using the router as a joiner

Cheapness is often the reason given for adopting a router and associated biscuit-joint cutters. It can be a solution, although a full-blown joiner is the best long-term answer. The router scores because it can operate in awkward situations such as on a longitudinally curved joint face, where a joiner might not slot to the right depth because of its flat faceplate.

The slots produced by a router, especially T-joint ones using a straight bit, are not ideal compared to a proper joiner blade, but nevertheless it has some good uses, possibly as a back-up to a standard biscuit joiner. The Triton swinging fence system (see chapter 1:4) uses an inverted static Triton router and a Triton biscuit cutter to create safe accurate joints using a special type of biscuit that matches the cutter shape.

The router is simply another string to the biscuit-jointing woodworker's bow.

TECHNIQUE:

Slotting with the router

Many amateur woodworkers choose not to invest in a full-blown biscuit joiner, using their existing router instead. Any lightweight router of about 650–850 watt power and a decent-sized cutter opening in the base is capable of using a biscuit cutter set. These come in two-, three- and four-blade types, the two-bladers being intended for lightweight craft use and perfectly acceptable for most purposes, unless you intend doing a lot of work in this way. The cutter comes mounted on an arbor with three interchangeable bearings which give the correct projection for each biscuit slot size. No other means of guidance is needed.

ABOVE There are various biscuit cutter sets on the market.

TECHNIQUE:

Slotting with the router

There is a definite difference in technique, because this time we are using a blade less than half the diameter of a joiner blade.

Fit the cutter, plunge to the correct depth so the slot will be centred on the board edge and lock in the plunged position. Where before you had just one biscuit mark you now need two, about ⅜–½in (10–12mm) apart so the blade can run along between the two to make the slot long enough. Obviously the slot is not the right shape in which to neatly fit the biscuit but it does work.

Plug in, rest the router on the board but out to the side, switch on and pull into the board edge and slide from left to right in the direction of the cutter. Work from the centre of one biscuit mark to the other, then withdraw the router to the side – do not unplunge while the cutter is in the board!

Move on to the next slot and so on. In practice it is quick and easy, and just a case of observing the same machining procedure all the time.

OPPOSITE, TOP Router biscuit jointing requires two marks per slot rather than just one with a dedicated biscuit joiner.

OPPOSITE, BOTTOM Routing biscuit slots is quick once you know the routine.

ABOVE A combination of worktop bolts and biscuits ensures very neat, almost invisible joints.

Because the arbor (shaft) of the cutter is not very long it is only possible to do edge to edge and corner joints, and not T joints or mitres, other than flat mitres. However, it is cheaper than buying separate jointing machine if you already own a router. There is even an advantage over the biscuit joiner, as the router can work tight into internal corners and along curved or 'doglegged' meeting surfaces. This makes it useful for unconventional furniture or the postformed joints in kitchen worktops.

A way around the T-joint or mitre problem can be to use a straight ³⁄₁₆in (4mm) two-flute cutter for the slots in the middle of a panel. The router in this situation can run against a T-square or a strip of wood acting as a fence. Each slot needs a second pass to loosen the tightly packed chippings and, of course, you will need to apply marks beforehand that will correspond to the length of slot required for the chosen biscuit size.

KEY POINT

However you use the router for biscuiting, the joiner is more versatile overall and where a slot created by the joiner matches the biscuit shape and ensures most glue is exuded when the joint is closed, router slots allow a reservoir of glue at each end of the slot which may hinder drying time, especially in cold, damp weather.

KEY POINT

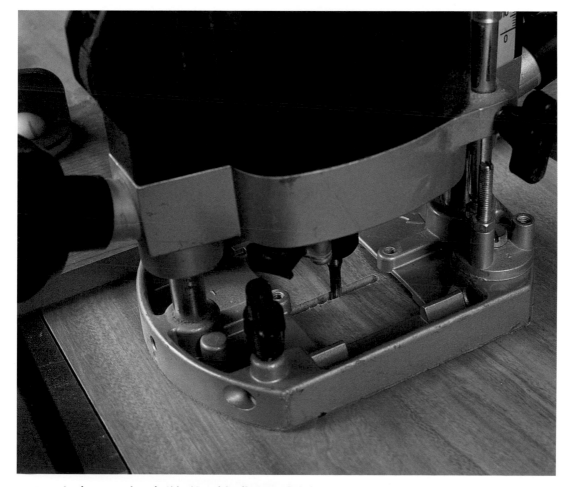

ABOVE As the cutter is only ³⁄₁₆in (4mm) in diameter, it is important to make several passes down to the final depth so that it does not get stressed and break.

2:5 Board sawing

Ordinarily the portable saw is used for board sawing unless you are lucky enough to own a professional panel saw. The biscuit joiner has a mini sawblade which can be used for the same purpose. It therefore allows one tool to do two different tasks: slotting and sawing. The DeWalt 685 is the only swing-down push-ahead model suited perfectly to sawing. However, by retracting anti-slip devices, an ordinary plunge model used with a straightedge, cramps and sawhorses, can be transformed into a quite accurate means of sawing down large 8ft × 4ft (2.4m × 1.2m) panels with ease. Since the *raison d'être* of the joiner is carcass work it is sensible to use it for preparing all the components before jointing them.

A spare blade is essential as wear will eventually set in and you will wish to keep one blade in good condition, if only for biscuit jointing work. Once again, the joiner demonstrates its inherent utility.

Some manufacturers of biscuit joiners put a safety warning in their instructions not to use the joiner as a saw. I don't blame them and perhaps they are right, but I've used various joiners like this for years without incident. Indeed the Bosch and DeWalt swing-down types are intended for sawing as well as biscuiting. The normal plunge joiner seems a less likely candidate but can be made to work in this mode without compromising safety. Why would we need a mini saw of this type? Well, an obvious reason is to cut man-made board – to a maximum depth of about ¾–⅞in (19–22mm) – where a large or expensive panel saw is usually necessary. It is also possible to cut grooves or even rebates with a bit of care (see chapter 2:6).

Method

Here's how to use the biscuit joiner for sawing. First of all make sure you have good extraction (this should be the case for most jointing work in any case) as the amount of dust produced is excessive. Having a spare blade is sensible as a lot of sawing will wear the tungsten carbide teeth, resulting in a visit to the saw doctor's. The DeWalt machine can take a slightly larger but thinner fine tooth designed for ply cutting; however, my own experience is that the standard joiner blade, being thicker, doesn't flex while cutting, which gives an uneven cut, unlike the thin blade which gives a neater, almost planed finish. Next, the board should be laid across sawhorses or a couple of workmates.

ABOVE Using a swing-down joiner to saw a board.

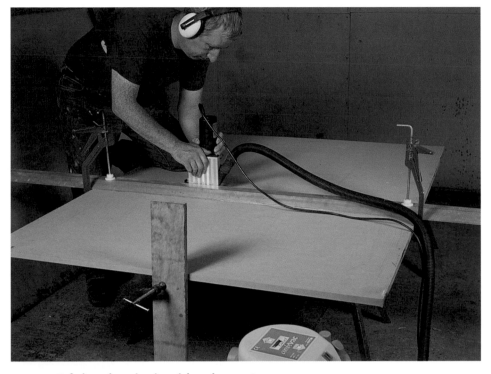

ABOVE Safe board sawing is quick and accurate.

If you don't want the top surfaces to get scarred by the projecting blade, place some scrap board on top of these supports.

Swing-down joiners

The swing-down type joiner goes into saw mode quickly: just unlock the motor body, swing down to the lowest setting and relock. This means you are pushing it from behind, which makes sense. A straightedge is needed – I favour a lightweight aluminium 'plasterer's feather-edge' that has one tapered edge and one vertical, which is the edge we will actually use. Measure the width you need, allowing slightly more so you can make a second cut afterwards in order to remove the

manufacturer's original edge (which tends to get tatty and damaged in transit). Now measure the offset distance between the blade and the edge of the joiner base that will run against the fence. Transfer this distance onto the board and place the straightedge on these new marks and cramp in position. The DeWalt allows the blade to be moved from side to side giving fine adjustment when sawing or biscuiting. Wearing personal dust protection and goggles, lean over the board, switch on the joiner, plunge and proceed to push it along the straightedge till the cut is done. So long as the blade projects through the board slightly, you will get two neat, well-sawn edges.

ABOVE **A good grip with the lower hand firmly on the loop handle is important when sawing with a plunge model.**

Straight-ahead joiners

The straight-ahead plunge-type machine is slightly more awkward to use. First retract any anti-slip devices (on some joiners this may not be possible), or you may be able to stick a piece of Formica on with double-sided tape through which the blade can be plunged for sawing. With the Draper (ex Ryobi), I have managed to unscrew the rubber-covered faceplate and fit an MDF replacement which gives enough 'slip'; however, this kind of conversion will not be approved by any manufacturer and you must be satisfied that it will not damage the machine or compromise your safety. If in doubt, don't do it!

As with all joiners you have the luxury of turning the machine on without it being plunged, so place it against the fence, switch on, then carefully plunge and, holding down (your choice of grip will make a difference – *never* hold the tail end of the motor housing on its own, hold the

KEY POINT

As a safety warning – never, ever unhook the return springs for sawing or grooving. This would allow the blade to slip in and out of the blade housing freely, and is therefore so dangerous it is not worth a moment's consideration.

move in the reverse direction as the machine may kickback, creating a hazard.

Although more care and effort is needed in keeping this type of joiner plunged and on course, it does work and for years I have used plunge joiners in saw mode when panel sawing. The blade can cause a certain amount of 'spelch' (breakout or tearing of wood fibres) so the best face should be underneath, with the tips of the teeth projecting through the board by just a couple of millimetres, which will reduce spelching to a minimum. This is really only a problem on cross-grain cutting.

joiner handgrip as well) against the pressure of the return springs, push it along the fence in the direction in which the blade is cutting and continue like this till the cut is done. Do not let the joiner

ABOVE Clean and spelched board side by side. The underside is normally the cleanest edge when sawing.

2:6 Making functional items

This chapter shows that the joiner, with a little imagination, can do tasks that you would normally expect from other tools and techniques. Drawer boxes and pulls are a doddle to do and make it easy to batch-produce drawers for carcass furniture such as a chest or cabinet. The ability to slot components in a sort of shallow saw mode means that discreet removable biscuits can be used for slide-on shelves that cannot possibly tip up if the shelf is loaded at the front or back edge. In the same vein, small sliding doors can be created or rebates cut, just by using the joiner set in shallow plunge mode and some common sense. When you are looking for a quick reliable ally in the workshop this is it. As usual it is only limited by the user's imagination.

Drawer pull

First up is the drawer pull and although you are limited to the maximum blade projection, and therefore the size of the pull, it is easy to do. Take your drawer front, cramp it down and draw a centre line. Now set the blade right up close to the fence (most fences either have a hole for the blade to safely push into or you may be able to stick an MDF sub-fence on, which won't matter if it does gets grazed by the blade). Line up the joiner's own centre mark exactly with the pencil line and plunge. Now move the fence up by a blade's width, line the joiner up again, plunge and continue like this until you have removed material to the full thickness of the board leaving a neat lemon-wedge-shaped cutout. All that remains is to sand the shape to remove the blade marks. This

makes a small but neat drawer pull. You can try plunging and moving between two strike marks to elongate the slot but more control is needed and the result probably won't be so neat.

ABOVE The final handgrip shape looks very neat once sanded.

ABOVE When cutting a drawer pull the blade needs to be very close to the fence without damaging it. It may be possible to fix a thin piece of MDF on with double-sided tape to avoid any marring of the fence surface.

Drawer boxes

The biscuit joiner can make a drawer (or drawer box as it is correctly known in woodworking) from start to finish – apart from the sanding.

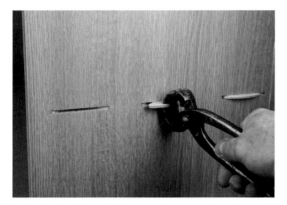

ABOVE Good old-fashioned pincers are ideal for extracting biscuits from slots.

Start by working out the drawer sizes to fit the carcass in question. You can buy modern 'easy runners' made from cream-white coated pressed steel and fitted with nylon rollers, from DIY stores. Allow for the width of these – about ½in (12.5mm) per side – and make each drawer shallower than the height of the space available by about $^{25}/_{32}$in (20mm) so the drawers can be hooked into the runners. Finally, allow for the thickness of the drawer front to be screwed on afterwards and also slightly less deep than the carcass.

Now sketch out your drawers so the sides run right through from front to back while the front and back sit inside the sides.

ABOVE Complete drawer box with easy-on runners.

ABOVE Machining the drawer bottom groove in two passes, using a ³⁄₃₂in (2mm) sheet of MDF on the second pass to create a ¼in (6mm) groove with the ³⁄₁₆in (4mm) joiner blade.

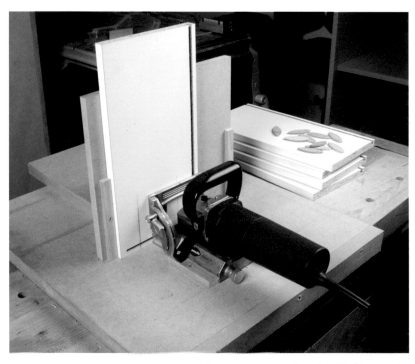

ABOVE Doing a test cut on the drawer front and back component jig. Note how the component will slide to one side to do the second slot.

The material thickness can vary but ½–⅝in (12–18mm) will allow for biscuits to be slotted in without penetrating through the drawer sides. Make up a jig specifically for making drawers, as shown in chapter 2:8. Note that for different drawer widths you will need to alter the jig to suit.

You are basically making up a mini carcass so the same care in organizing and marking up parts is needed. Start by doing the drawer bottom grooves. The easiest way is to use an L-jig, cramping each drawer component to it in turn. Set the blade depth for about a ¼in (6mm) projection.

If the setting dial doesn't allow this you can alter the fine adjuster (but don't forget to reset it when you go back to regular

RIGHT The drawer side jig in use. Again the component needs to move over for the second slot.

biscuiting). By sitting the joiner on a reference board the first pass will be about ⁵⁄₁₆–³⁄₈in (8–10mm) up from the bottom edge, then proceed to groove, moving the joiner from left to right in the direction of cut. Two passes at different fence settings are required to get a ¼in (6mm)-wide groove so do all components at one setting, then machine them all again after placing a ³⁄₃₂in (2mm) MDF packer under the joiner. Proceed to biscuit slot all the same parts in one go (front and back) before altering the setup for the other joint halves (sides).

Obviously the biscuits which hold the drawer box together mustn't project into the space where the drawer bottom groove is. Dry assemble a drawer in order to work out the size of the drawer bottoms. Saw these out with the joiner and then assemble each drawer in turn using a reasonable but not excessive amount of glue. Cramp carefully, check for square and leave to dry. The drawer front is an entirely separate item to be considered afterwards although you need to allow for its size in your overall calculations.

RIGHT The partly assembled drawer box showing the joint detail.

Sliding doors

Small sliding doors are quite easy to make using biscuits as the runners. Let's assume you have a frame for the doors to fit in. Now set the joiner to groove (as in saw mode) so that you end up with two grooves in the top and bottom of the frame. Each groove will take one door (for a two-door set or if you have an extra long cupboard, three doors in total). Check that both doors will slide past each other with a gap between. Now plunge and cut each groove in turn, making sure the joiner is held level as you move along so the grooves remain straight. Note that the grooves do not need to go right from one end of the frame to the other, so long as the biscuits in the doors are set in from each end of the door. Fold some abrasive and lightly sand the sides of the grooves to remove any roughness that will hamper free-running. Now cut the doors to fit loosely from top to bottom and to overlap each other when closed. Put strike marks a short way in from each side of the doors, top and bottom. Set the joiner fence so the slots will be in a suitable position to allow the doors to clear each other when they slide past. Set a plunge depth for size 10 biscuits and make the bottom slots; reset for size 20s and do the top slots. Glue and fit the right size biscuits in their respective slots, cleaning off any excess. When dry, sand each projecting biscuit so it tapers in profile slightly, towards the top exposed

ABOVE Grooving the assembled frame for sliding doors; the frame must be wide enough to allow doors to pass each other.

ABOVE Once sanded to a taper and waxed, these door runner biscuits will allow the doors to move quite easily.

ABOVE Glazed sliding door fitted into unfinished frame, the top size 10 biscuit visible.

Slide-on shelves

These are useful when some shelves may need to be added or removed as storage requirements change.

Whereas fixed shelves are biscuited on with glue, in this case the biscuits remain in the carcass and don't even have to be glued, while the shelves have their ends grooved so they can slide onto the fixed biscuits. When grooving the shelf ends keep the joiner level or use a reference board to ensure the groove stays straight and stops just short of the front edge so no unsightly slot shows. To assist in removal or fitment, the exposed part of the carcass biscuits can be sanded to taper them or the slot sanded to ease the fit. If the biscuits are not glued, they can always be pulled out with pincers leaving a neat slot behind.

edge of the biscuit. Wax the biscuits, lower door edges and frame grooves to help the doors slide, then push each door in turn upwards into the top slot and clip the lower biscuits into the bottom grooves. As the doors drop, the smaller lower biscuits fit fully in the grooves while the larger upper biscuits still project enough into the upper grooves to stay in place.

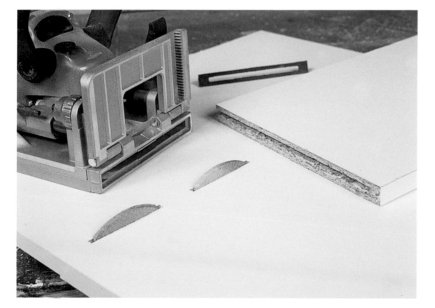

LEFT Neat and discreet shelf fixing that is removable.

Cable access

This is useful for furniture on which you might have a computer or phone, fax and answerphone. The wiring can be excessive so a biscuit-jointed cable trough underneath can be used to hold all the wires, but with a means of getting to all the devices.

Cramp a jig board with a suitably-sized recess onto the top of the carcass; this recess will act both as a fence and end stops for the joiner in saw mode. Plunge and do one pass, then move the jig forward by a blade's width ensuring that the end of the jig follows a line marked on the top of the furniture, so the ends of the cutout are neat and level. Repeat this

LEFT Shows how the cable access cover can hide all the wiring. The slot is wide enough for the wires to be hidden underneath in a cable trough.

LEFT Cutout jig being used to make the opening; it is moved slightly to make each new cut.

ABOVE The finished lid with bevelled ends underneath.

ABOVE The lid supports keep the lid flush on the top surface.

operation until you have a cutout with dished ends that is about 2–3in (50–75mm) wide. Sand the dished surfaces smooth. Then cut an infill piece with matching grain and make it slightly shorter than the recess so the wires can come out at the ends. Round the underside at both ends to match the dished shape of the recess. This can be done on a bandsaw or belt sander and then with a careful hand sanding to get a smooth finish. Lastly, glue and pin a small strip under each side of the recess so this cover or infill piece is held level with the surrounding wood.

Rebate

Small rebates, such as for holding panels on the back of furniture, are easy to do with the biscuit joiner. Work out the profile measurement of the rebate and set the depth for cutting into the edge (you may need to turn the fine adjuster to get an exact setting). Move the fence so the distance from that to the bottom edge of the blade is the rebate width. Machine from the edge because the joiner fence will need as much support as possible – if it is done from the face first this might not give such support on the edge cut afterwards. Cramp the board down on the bench for this operation. Plunge and do a groove along the board edge.

Now put the board upright in the vice and reset the joiner to make the other groove. Keep the joiner steady and true because this second cut removes a narrow strip of wood which the joiner was using for support; if necessary cramp a longer board flush with the top to extend the running surface.

A better result can be achieved by using an L-jig but this time the section to be rebated will rest on the reference board and a packer may be needed to get the correct rebate size. A very small rebate could be done from the face side in only one or two passes, thus avoiding a lot of resetting, and will make only sawdust.

ABOVE Cutting a rebate with a biscuit joiner is a good substitute for a router and rebate cutter.

Kerfing

A 'kerf' is the path or slot cut by any sawblade. In the case of a biscuit joiner in saw mode, it is a slot ⁵⁄₃₂in (4mm) wide by whatever depth it is set to or is capable of (unless using the DeWalt swing-down model and optional thin ply-cutting blade).

In antique furniture restoration, warped table tops are often kerfed repeatedly on the underside and the resulting slots have new thicker strips of wood glued in to try and persuade the warped top to flatten out. I didn't find this very successful when I worked in antique restoration and indeed

I know of a restorer who has instead developed a highly successful router technique which entails removing almost the entire underside! I don't think a biscuit joiner will do this any better than a circular saw can.

Here is a better use for kerfing with the joiner. Nowadays you can buy flexible MDF board that can be bent into almost any configuration including quite tight radii. It is expensive in the UK and available on special order only, but if you want to create a smooth curve such as the modern chair design shown on the next page, it could not be easier.

ABOVE Hand pressure is used to hold the T-square in position as it has to be moved quickly between cuts. Note the adjustable screw for sighting down, to get the correct spacing.

Cut a ¼in (6mm)-thick board oversize for trimming later on and place on a sacrificial board with a strip of wood at the back to stop the MDF slipping around. Cramp a joiner T-square (project 3:1) onto the MDF workpiece leaving room for the joiner to sit at one end. Set to the correct cut depth, which will be nearly three-quarters of the material thickness. Use in saw mode to make the first slot. Re-cramp the T-square a suitable distance away from the first slot to create the next one – slots shouldn't be more than ¼–⁵⁄₁₆in (6–7mm) apart.

To make for quick, accurate slot setting, rather than pre-marking them all with a ruler, have an adjustable screw on the T-square that projects towards the joiner side by the required distance. If it is low down enough it won't get cut by the joiner with each pass. You will be able to sight down the screw head and set the T-square accordingly. I would suggest that you use two thin kerfed boards with the kerfs facing each other and glue in between for a much stronger, reliable result rather than just one thickness, as the slotted MDF surface can break up easily. A gap-filling glue such as Extramite or polyurethane is best. You can easily create all kinds of interesting modern designs using this technique.

ABOVE A very flexible result!

ABOVE This chair will have a second kerfed layer glued face-to-face with the first layer. (Courtesy of Mark Cass, editor of *New Woodworking*.)

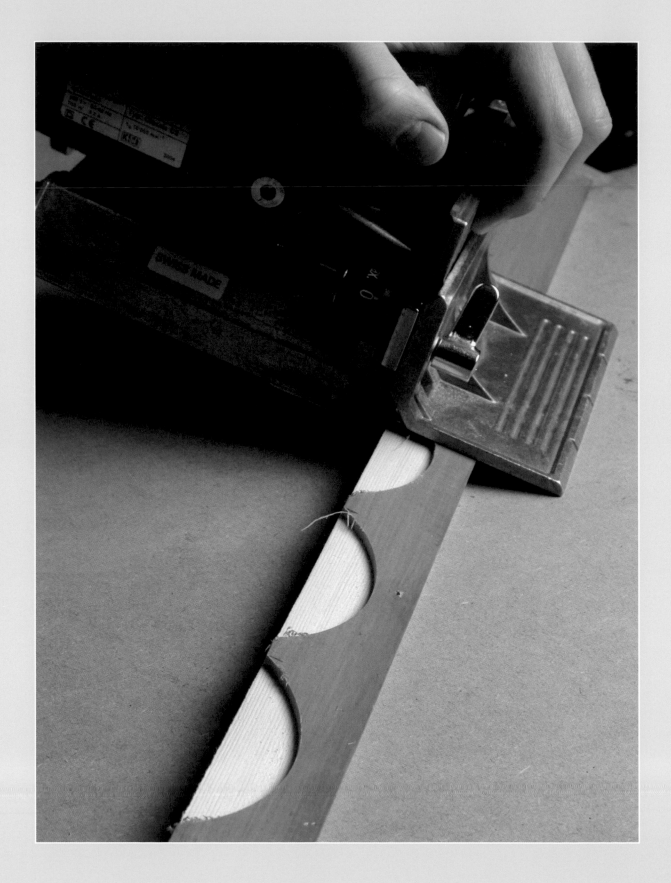

2:7 Decorative joiner work

No one, least of all me, would pretend that the biscuit joiner was
the ideal machine for creating decorative effects. However the
effects described in this chapter are effective, easy to produce
and quite appealing. They are more appropriate for modern style
furniture but are fun to do and, unlike a router, do not require
any special cutters.

An ordinary board edge can look plain, square and bland but
three or more passes with a joiner can create an interesting
multi-grooved effect that looks good and is also pleasant to the
touch once lightly sanded. A traditional-style dresser or shelves
could benefit from the 'blind' or through scallop effect. It is one
joiner-produced effect that does suit a traditional piece and cannot
be created adequately by any other means. I'm sure there is still
scope for further experimentation and readers may surprise me
and themselves by creating still more decorative touches.

ABOVE Fluting outer slots of column.

ABOVE The finished fluted column: ready for a coat of sanding sealer and for fitting to a bookcase.

Fluted column

The fluted or reeded column dates back to classical architecture. It consists of a number of half-round profile slots in wood or stone which finish with a rounded dished shape at each slot end. Our variant is created by running the joiner along at different fence settings to groove the board repeatedly, each groove next to the last giving the slot effect; and several slots together creating a wider 'flute' shape. Starting and stopping the joiner at accurate pencil-marked lines is important so that you get a neat dished 'sweep' at the end of the slot. Even so, the use of a sharp chisel and some abrasive will be needed to clean it up a little.

Generally a fluted column would be between two and five slots wide. Therefore if you have two or more columns to a piece of furniture you can do all the outer slots first by turning each workpiece over, then the inner slots in succession likewise. As always with any tricky piece of work, use a test piece to get all the settings right before attacking the actual job itself.

You can hold the joiner to the test piece with the motor off and adjust the fence to just fit in each side of the slots so it acts as 'reference' for transferring the settings to the actual job. As always with sawing and grooving, the anti-slip devices need to be retracted or removed. Once completed to your satisfaction, these columns can be biscuited to the carcass taking care that the biscuits on the back don't penetrate through the slots on the front. Alternatively you can run the slots right through and finish the columns off with a plain larger block at the bottom and a moulding at the top.

Multiple groove effect

This effect is useful for table edges and the like. Cramp the table top down, adjust the joiner for a suitable but not excessive cut depth, a fence-to-blade distance of about ³⁄₁₆–⁷⁄₃₂in (4–5mm), and retract anti-slip devices. Then, holding the machine level and with plenty of downward pressure on the fence, plunge and proceed to groove in the direction of cut. If the table top can overhang two sides of your work support, you can groove both of these sides before having to uncramp it and turn it round to do the other sides. Reset the fence for the next groove allowing a minimum space of ⅛in (3mm) between grooves so the remaining wood is strong enough. Repeat as many times as the thickness of the wood allows; in ⁵⁄₈–³⁄₄in (18–20mm) material this means just two grooves but it still looks good. The top ³⁄₁₆–⁷⁄₃₂in (4–5mm) of material allows the top edge to be rounded over slightly with a bit of hand-applied abrasive paper.

⬤KEY POINT

A table top with rounded or 'chopped' (angled) corners looks even better with a multiple groove effect if you are after a designer-looking piece of furniture. It adds detail and interest quickly and easily, and it looks impressive too!

⬤KEY POINT

ABOVE A modern style, bevelled and grooved table edge.

Star detail

I used this detail on an MDF coffee table a few years ago. It is best used as an applied block to a larger surface because a bit of trial and error is involved and it's better not to experiment on your nicely put together furniture. Instead work this idea into the overall design if you think there is a suitable place for it. Typically this might be corner detail, perhaps on the underframe of a table or at the ends of a frieze rail, just below a cornice at the top of a bookcase.

ABOVE Not everyone wants plain MDF with this effect. Veneered MDF looks more natural when applied to a piece of furniture.

Solid wood is not so suitable as it may start to fall apart, the more slots you do. MDF seems to fare best as it has no short grain to worry about, being formed from a series of compressed sheets of wood-based material and resin. Mark out a series of squares of the required size on a largish piece of MDF. A ⅝in (18mm) thickness is best; thinner sizes will need a smaller blade projection (resulting in a smaller star effect) or else the blade can be allowed to cut right through. Draw lines from corner to corner and across the middle of each square, then bisect each division again with a line (a protractor may help in setting these sub-divisions out). This number of lines will allow as many slots as possible without the whole thing becoming a mess. You need a mark at each side of the blade housing that shows the centre of the blade kerf (slot); some joiners actually have this marked, though it may not be very clear.

Now sit the joiner centred on one drawn line on the board and also centred across the line perpendicular to it. This must be done carefully for a neat result; plunge slowly and let the blade retract then swap around to the perpendicular line and repeat the operation. Note that no fence is used and it is entirely freehand, so do not place your hand near the bottom end of the machine for safety. Next, start on the major sub-divisions and lastly the minor ones. The more cuts you do, the harder it becomes to line the joiner up in both directions, as the guide lines get machined away. However you can sight along the outer part of each line for guidance – there is a bit of luck involved which is why you should allow more than you need – then select the best ones and cut them out afterwards. Lastly, sand the edges of the blocks and glue and 'rub' them into position. This creates a suction effect and should be enough to hold each block in place till dry, providing the blocks are lying down so they can't slip off.

ABOVE Note the setting out lines for the star detail. As more lines are cut it is harder to line up the joiner accurately.

KEY POINT

If your joiner lacks kerf centreline marks you can add them by placing a strip of masking tape along the base (with the machine unplugged), lining it up carefully with the centre of the blade from end to end, then pressing the tape in place. Now use a Stanley knife (box cutter) and a safety straightedge (one with a high edge that the blade cannot ride up over, to prevent injury) to cut into the alloy casing at each end using the tape line underneath to determine the cut line. The result is a thin but definite line at each end, and if the casing is silver or plain aluminium it can have black paint or a fine felt tip pen rubbed into the cuts to highlight them against the bright finish. Remove the tape and your joiner now has another means of precise slot placement.

KEY POINT

LEFT Most joiner housings are alloy and therefore easy to knife-cut a kerf mark on.

Groove highlight detail

This is covered in detail in chapter 2:3 under boxed-up joints. It can be used to disguise a joint or highlight the difference between two flush surfaces – say a table top that is flush to the underframe or similarly, the top of a cabinet. In other words, use to add a little bit of detail

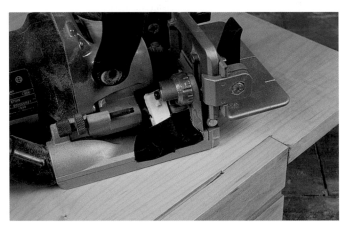

ABOVE Grooving on a boxed-up joint helps disguise it.

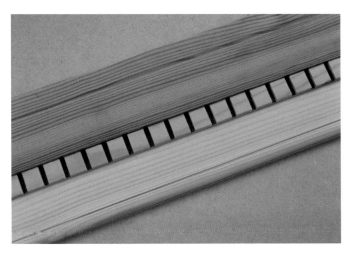

ABOVE Dentil moulding makes a definite difference to a standard moulded profile.

where none exists or where cross-grain wood meets the long grain and might otherwise look a bit odd.

Dentil moulding

This is a traditional effect that adds a bit of grandeur to a piece when added to other mouldings. Fire surrounds, cabinets and so on, will all benefit from this moulding. The jig needed is covered in chapter 2:8, and basically the joiner sits fixed over two boards between which the strip to be moulded slides under the joiner. A succession of slots at pre-determined intervals produces the required dentil or toothed effect quickly and easily. Afterwards it simply needs to be cut, pinned and glued in place on the furniture.

Slotted frieze

This is rather more interesting than a plain rail on a table underframe or frieze rail on a cabinet. The setup which is detailed in chapter 2:8 is similar to the dentil moulding jig only this time it must accommodate a piece of wood up to about 2in (50mm) wide – if you are happy with a plain strip along the top edge, 3⅛in (80mm) wide is possible – and the groove spacing is closer. The maximum depth of cut is needed to slot the full width of the workpiece properly; the slight curve to the bottom of each groove isn't very noticeable.

Through and blind scallops

These can be used on both modern and traditional furniture, are easy to do and turn a plain shelf into a much more pleasing one. Put overall shelf end marks on the face of a piece of solid wood, left overlength, for guiding the joiner. Then place strike marks all the way along, in between the end marks using equal sub-divisions. You can work this out using a calculator to get the exact spacings. Note that for a blind scallop you may need slightly thicker material; a through scallop only needs thin stuff. Now, as for the drawer pull, start with the fence set right on the blade for the first cut, do all the scallops and reset the blade for the next, lower pass and recut. If a blind scallop is required just two or three passes are needed. With a through scallop, keep

ABOVE This slotted frieze will be stained to match the mahogany of this side table and once done it will be hard to tell it is MDF!

cutting in successive passes until you have gone right through the thickness of the material. Sand all the scallops, trim to length and pin and glue to the shelf edge. Thick stock can then be biscuited on, with size 0 biscuits, of course!

ABOVE The blind scallop has strength but still looks good.

ABOVE Through scalloped edging is more delicate in appearance.

2:8 Jigs and setups

I am a firm believer in the use of jigs and static setups. They are much more controllable than freehand working and accurate repetition operations are easily achievable. It is also safer because both machine and component are fixed or at least held in a precise location while machining. It costs very little to make a jig – offcuts of MDF or ply are generally used, plus a few screws, fixing blocks and shim material.

The L-jig in particular turns the component into the vertical axis perpendicular to a reference board so that precise slotting of face surfaces can be done. This is required for drawer boxes, for example. Ordinarily standing a workpiece on end without support would be disastrous because of the lack of control but the L-jig avoids that difficulty. Tedious jobs like slotting the ends of bed slats which are narrow and present endgrain to the cutter (and are therefore risky as well), suddenly become safe, quick and fast to do. Such is the versatility of the biscuit joiner even when fixed firmly down.

L-jig

The L-jig is a basic step away from using the joiner on its own. It allows jointing work to be done with precision especially on large sections. Make up a biscuited MDF L-shape at exactly 90°, large enough for the jointing you wish to do. Fix it down to your reference board so there is space in front for the joiner (or workpiece) to sit. Providing the components are not too long, they can be stood up against the jig and the joiner can sit directly on the reference board or on packers if the slots are going to be too low down.

If the components are large it is better to lie them down and place the joiner vertically against the L-jig. The effect is the same, it's just a matter of choice. Always cramp the workpiece before biscuiting. You can fit side stops against which the joiner can press, thus determining the outer biscuit slot positions without having to mark them out, although this is only really worthwhile if you have a lot of identical components or you can fix the joiner down and move the workpiece across instead. The L-jig is also very useful for the safe, quick jointing of mouldings, ready to apply to a carcass.

LEFT An L-jig in use.

ABOVE The biscuit joiner fixed down. The rear of the L-jig has stops fixed at each side.

Drawer jig

This is essentially like the L-jig with slight additions; each drawer size will need the jig to be altered accordingly.

The joiner needs to be fixed down. Fit a stop at the right so the joiner is automatically positioned for the left slot, and vice versa but leaving less distance so the second biscuit is offset away from the edge, thus leaving it clear of the bottom panel groove. Remove the L-piece and adapt the reference base of the jig which will allow the other half of the joint, the ends of the component to be machined. Note that this cuts either the left-hand or right-hand joint only (because of the bottom panel). You will need to move the stop blocks to do the 'other hand' of the joint. This setup is easier to put together than it sounds and providing you mark and stack your components correctly, it works a treat.

ABOVE The resulting joint, using just one biscuit per corner as it is a shallow drawer.

127

Bed slat jig

Narrow components are too dangerous to slot at the ends without fixing the workpiece and/or the joiner in position with some extra means of support as well. The slots can be off-centre and show too much at the sides and not line up properly on assembly; in addition each one needs to be marked up, which takes time. A simple jig takes care of all this for you. A typical use is for fixing bed slats, where on average about 52 slats (that's 104 joints) need to be cut per bed. No doubt there are other uses for this type of jig as well.

Choose a long board that will accommodate both joiner and workpiece.

⊙ KEY POINT

Fix your joiner down as previously mentioned. This isn't as difficult as it sounds. Some joiners come with a couple of fixing holes but these are not adequate on their own. Use short strips of wood to frame the joiner body without obstructing either the extraction port or its ability to plunge. Then add more pieces on top to hold the body down.

⊙ KEY POINT

Plastic 'modesty' blocks used for fixing panel furniture together also make a quick and easy means of securing your joiner with use of screws.

ABOVE A slat jig is easy to knock up and can be kept for future use.

Once you are satisfied the joiner can't move at all, screw two long strips at 90° to the fence, just far apart enough for the workpiece to fit in the middle, and centred on the blade, of course. If all the components are identical in width they should fit snugly between these two strips. Now put the stack of parts near to hand and push one up to the faceplate with the joiner switched on, plunge the joiner with the other hand and repeat at the other end of the workpiece keeping it the same way up so the slots are level with each other. Do this as many times as necessary – after the first few it becomes very quick indeed but rather boring!

Framing cam jig

Framing for pictures and mirrors needs to be held firmly but also released quickly between cuts. It must also accommodate different width stock. This jig does both left- and right-hand mitres by swapping the position of the biscuit joiner. Check the angles of the strips and blocks carefully before using in earnest, though the angle at which you cut your mitres is most important of all. The cam allows sufficient quick pressure to be applied and released, making fast working possible.

ABOVE A slat pushed up to the joiner with the finished article in front; fast and safe to use.

ABOVE A framing cam jig is simple to make, and will speed up frame making if you have a lot of joints.

129

Dentil mould and slotted frieze jig

The jigs for these two operations are similar, though you will need one for each if you choose to do both. Another simple setup, it needs two strips of wood either side of the workpiece and should be a fraction higher (pieces of veneer edging tape are useful for this). Fix the joiner between strips of wood which are exactly 90° to the other pieces and add more to hold the joiner down. Make a test cut with the blade set to the chosen depth. Mark next to it where the next slot should be.

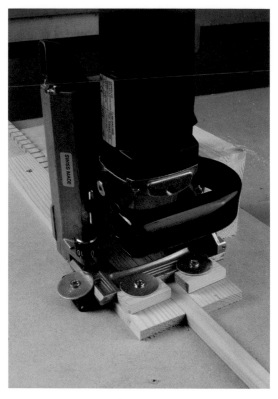

ABOVE Ingenuity in fixing down the joiner may be required.

In the case of dentil moulding this should be sufficiently clear of the joiner to mark in pen on the guide pieces at the side. Each time you do a slot, pull the wood along until that slot lines up with your marks, then plunge again and repeat ad infinitum.

For the slotted frieze, the jig has to accommodate wider strips and the slots are also very close together. On the DeWalt swing-down model this isn't a problem because the blade can be moved close to the edge of the housing, then you can sight down the housing for each successive slot position. You may be able

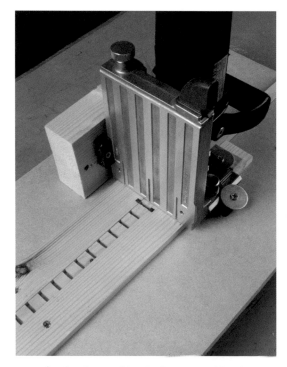

ABOVE The slot position is determined by the markings on the jig. As the strip is pushed through, each new slot is lined up to the marks before cutting the next one.

(KEY POINT

Drop a biscuit into each emerging slot with it resting against the baseplate or partly into a slot in one of the guide strips to get precise spacing, or else fit a thin alloy strip to the jig to do the same job, either with the dentil moulding or frieze rail.

to do this with your joiner anyway. If you can't, it may be a case of marking the first few slot positions on the workpiece accurately and lining up against an arbitrary mark on one of the guide pieces near the blade housing on the feed side. Once the slotted strip starts to emerge on the other side, make new marks on the guide strip on the outfeed side and use those to ensure accurate repetition slotting.

(KEY POINT

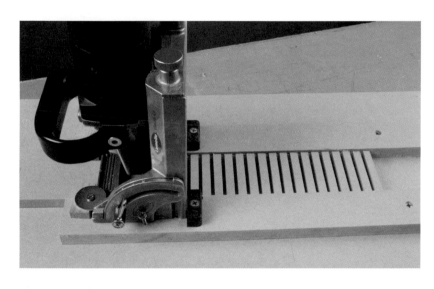

LEFT Looking from the sighting position down the edge of joiner when frieze cutting.

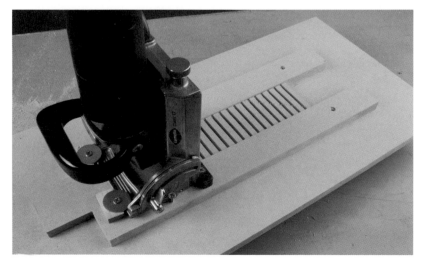

LEFT Screws, washers and modesty blocks locate the joiner firmly in the right place on the jig.

2:9 Working examples

Site work or DIY tasks around the home can benefit from the lightweight portable nature of the biscuit joiner and its inherent accuracy compared to some power tools such as the power drill, which has to be 'steered' to try and keep it straight and with no proper means of limiting its depth of cut. Fitting out kitchens can be difficult at the best of times but key operations like fitting and jointing worktops, upstands and decor panels in situ are made easier and more precise using a joiner and without any visible fixings at all.

Working on existing furniture, say to remove a back panel, is really easy because the joiner can follow the inside of a carcass or a suitable straightedge, whereas a jigsaw will invariably wander even when following a drawn line. Yet again we have invested in a tool capable of far more than its simple design and construction would suggest.

It isn't obvious what the joiner can do in practice apart from the new jointwork that we have already discussed, so here are a few of the more interesting examples.

Old and antique furniture

I wouldn't like to suggest that power tools and antiques mix, clearly they don't. The careful considered use of hand tools and proper restoration materials are essential if old, much-loved pieces of furniture or possibly quite valuable antique examples are not to be ruined. However, during the time that I ran an antique restoration business I came up against a recurring problem: how to rejoin separated boards

ABOVE Two pieces of French-polished, walnut-veneered solid wood ready for jointing. Protective masking tape has been applied with strike marks.

on table tops. These could be solid oak, ash or mahogany drop-leaf or Pembroke tables. The conventional answer usually meant cleaning the animal glue off the edges, hand planing until true and remaking these butt joints. In some cases planing edges would not be desirable as it would spoil the look of a long-since opened-up top, but some means of jointing was still required. Inserting a loose, glued tongue wasn't an option since it meant running the boards over a sawtable with consequent damage to the boards and possibly the operator too. The old pocketed screw fixings or glue blocks underneath were reused, thus holding the top in a fixed position that wouldn't allow for further shrinkage, which could therefore precipitate joint failure again.

As I have already mentioned I joined an interior design company as a cabinetmaker, which was the first time I set eyes on a biscuit joiner. Its apparent lack of intrusive machining, coupled with the ability to work on an uneven edge and still give good alignment seemed to have the potential for making a better joint – along the lines of a loose tongue, which even if it parted a little would still hold good, just exposing a bit of each biscuit (which can be stained dark to be less noticeable). It seems I wasn't alone in thinking this and I have since met several cabinetmakers or restorers who use a biscuit joiner for just this function.

TECHNIQUE:

Jointing table top boards

TECHNIQUE:

Jointing table top boards

Where safe, practical or necessary, true the edges with a hand plane, but use your judgement here (they may also need cleaning off first). Next lay each board in the original order and apply masking tape along the top close to each edge. (Note that the tape should not be pressed down too firmly, to avoid pulling any finish off when the tape is lifted.) The tape is needed to rest the joiner fence on without marking the finish and to mark out the biscuit positions without causing damage. Even so, you must still use light pen or pencil pressure, or slight dents will result and these will show if the table surface is viewed against the light. Proceed to slot the edges taking care that the joiner is presented level with the boards – any misalignment may be obvious and cannot be removed by sanding!

Use either glued or dry biscuits depending on the particular requirement. Lift the tape carefully afterwards and if the finish is disturbed be very circumspect about how you treat it. Generally nothing more than an application of a hardening wax polish is acceptable.

It is sometimes possible to carry out this machining with half the table top still fixed to its underframe. This avoids damaging any rusted-in screws or firmly fixed glue blocks. In this case the joiner can sit in the open space in the middle of the frame. If you are not confident about using this repair technique, don't do it, as any resultant damage will spoil and devalue the piece of furniture.

Removing carcass back panels

I worked for a bespoke kitchen company for a while and installed a number of kitchens or 'snagged' others (snagging refers to corrections, finishing or improvements needed after installation), often at the client's request. One such kitchen needed a hi-fi unit installed in a large island unit in the centre of the kitchen. This entailed cutting out a back panel in one side of the unit, which is difficult at the best of times, because a jigsaw can't get close to the carcass sides and leaves

a ragged cut. Hand sawing with a keyhole saw is even more impractical. Worse still, I was told to expect some mains wiring hanging just behind the panel, posing a high risk if the cutting out went wrong! The solution in this case was to use a normal straight-ahead-type plunge biscuit joiner equipped with efficient dust extraction set to a very shallow cut depth without its fence on. The back panel thickness wasn't known for certain, though I could have hazarded a guess based on the standard board thicknesses that we used. I set the cut depth for just over $\frac{5}{16}$in (7mm), as this

KEY POINT

was the minimum carcass back thickness including the veneer applied to both faces. I then pressed the underside of the joiner against one carcass side in the corner, plunged and ran along sawing through the board till the other end was reached. This wasn't enough to penetrate so I set it for just over ⅜in (10mm), this being the next likely board thickness. This time the blade just went through the board, and I repeated this around all four sides, until the panel was just fixed at the corners where the blade couldn't reach. This last job was done with a keyhole saw, taking care not to let the blade go in very far. Finally the panel dropped away revealing . . . nothing! In fact the wiring was off to one side and didn't pose a risk, but by

KEY POINT

As usual, with any of the operations discussed in this book, it isn't our intention to suggest practices that are at all dangerous. On most occasions, the removal of in-situ back panels and so on doesn't include the extra problem of wiring, but is simply to facilitate altering a piece of furniture to suit a new use. Always consider properly any intended machining operation you do, and that way you should stay safe!

using the joiner, with its precise depth setting, meant that I could work 'blind' in relative safety.

ABOVE A knob was removed from the joiner to get closer to the corner, with a Japanese-style pullsaw being used to complete the cut.

Kitchen cabinet and worktop installation

The biscuit is ideal for kitchens and wardrobes. Cupboard carcasses can be biscuited together, though they are usually made from melamine-faced chipboard or MDF which doesn't stick together. Don't rely on biscuits alone; use modern twinfast screws in between for extra strength, while the biscuits are a good locational aid.

Often 'decor panels', which are solid wood or veneered facings for cabinet ends are fitted to cover up the melamine on the outside. This is a natural job for the biscuit and should be done once the cabinets are fitted and after the decor panels have been trimmed to fit.

Modern kitchens often have lighting fitted under the top wall-hung cabinets. This needs to be hidden with a lighting pelmet. This is made from solid wood, often has a moulded lower edge and is mitred at the front corners. Here the joiner can be applied from underneath the cabinet using the fence, then into the top edge of the pelmet and the two biscuited together. Some lightweight cramps can be used to hold the pelmet on firmly until the glue has dried.

Kitchen worktops need to finish neatly against the wall or have tiles fixed to them. A line of mastic is a messy answer and it

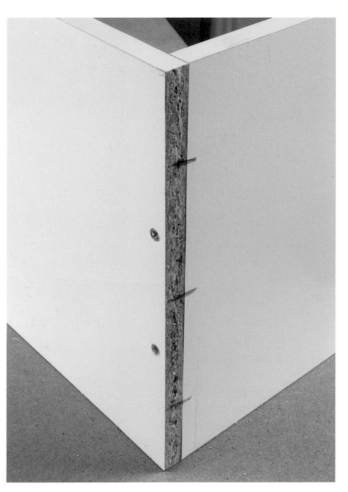

ABOVE The use of screws makes up for lack of good glue adhesion with melamine and chipboard.

ABOVE The decor panel projects forward flush with the doors when they are fitted.

RIGHT Once sealed and waxed, the lighting pelmet will blend well with the decor panel and doors (cabinet shown tilted back).

BELOW The packer against the wall ensures the slots are not too close to the worktop rear edge. Note the slot in the end of the upstand to help align the next piece, and the protective board in front to avoid marking the new worktop.

can become mouldy in time, as the silicone denaturizes. A better answer is to have an upstand piece of wood along the back edge of the worktop. This can be moulded slightly (not much as it may attract dust and dirt) and biscuited down into the worktop – provided it is made of wood or standard postform chipboard and laminate. Generally it is possible to place the joiner straight against the wall and slot near the back edge of the worktop. However, if there is a bit of a gap at the back edge, the slots may be only half-formed and the upstand may have nothing to fit into. In this case it may be possible to

press the joiner against a thin packing piece of ply, for example, thus offsetting the slots away from the wall. In any case the upstand should have its own slots slightly offset so it will be very slightly away from the wall. The reason is that walls are rarely flat and the upstand won't fit the biscuit slots because of the wall undulations. An offcut of upstand should be used to check the fit first.

Worktop joints

Standard postform worktop joints can be machined using a large router and a

ABOVE An open postform joint showing biscuits in the joint edge. When placed the right way up, there is no evidence of joint fixing.

home-made jig (there is more on this subject and making kitchen carcasses in my first book, *Routing for Beginners*. I won't go into the whole procedure of jointing worktops as it involves the router more than the joiner. However, it is worth pointing out that whereas special worktop bolts are used to pull the joint tightly together, there is nothing stopping it from sliding up or down so the surfaces can come out of alignment. The biscuit is a brilliantly simple way to solve this problem and three or four placed in between the bolt positions will do the trick. If you have a router biscuit-cutter set, you can even slot the last, dogleg section at the front, which a biscuit joiner cannot do.

Trimming skirtings and doors

Another example of site work with the joiner is trimming woodwork in situ. An obvious example would be skirting boards. In a 'proper' room situation, skirting should actually be fitted above the floorboards leaving an even 'carpet gap' underneath, rather than sitting it straight to the floor as usually happens. This carpet gap allows a carpet fitter to insert the carpet (not usually the underlay) under the skirting resulting in a very neat, smooth draughtproof carpet installation. If you want to emulate this technique then the biscuit joiner will allow you to do this. Skirting board is normally at least ¾in

(19mm) thick which comes within the scope of many joiners. The swing-down type is best because of its 'push along action' along the skirting. The floorboards may be uneven so you need to ensure they are well fixed down and lay a thin ply or hardboard over for the machine to slide on. Keep a spare blade handy in case you hit any screws or nails.

Doors can be treated in the same way, however since the maximum blade projection is barely half the thickness of an interior door a pass from each side will be needed. Another consideration is that doors need trimming because they are already sitting on the carpet too tightly. Trying to trim the bottom off the door from two sides can be difficult even though the joiner will be lying on a thin board for smooth running. The Lamello Tanga is a more reliable, but expensive, professional answer with its huge 7⅛in (180mm) diameter. trimming saw blade! However, it is worth giving the joiner a chance, before removing the door to trim in a more conventional way, as it is certainly quick.

These are just a few examples of how to put the joiner to work in awkward or unusual situations rather than just straightforward carcass building. The joiner is extra versatile and makes a very handy site tool!

ABOVE A cupboard door being trimmed in situ on a hardwood floor, to create a gap for carpet to be laid.

Fitting skirting to room panelling

A few years ago I was asked to fit out a study with maple panelling, then fit a matching skirting and dado rail to it. In the end I opted to use maple veneer MDF for all the flat areas and solid maple for the mouldings. All the panelling had to be made to length and pre-finished to a dark honey colour using spray lacquer. Since the high moulded skirting and dado rail had to be invisibly fixed, biscuit jointing was the natural answer. The biscuit slots around the top of the panelling were done before installation. Once the panelling was fixed to the walls the dado could be mitred to fit between walls, then slotted to match the slots on each respective piece of panelling. It was then glued and biscuited in place and because the room wasn't too large it was possible to 'spring' some softwood battens in between opposing panelled walls with protective pads at each end in order to hold the dado mouldings tight to the panels until the glue dried. The panelling wasn't pre-slotted for the skirting because I knew the floor was uneven and varied in height, so I felt it was better to see what the best installation height was once the panelling had been levelled up and fitted in place. The skirting was 6in (150mm) high overall with the moulded top section being about 1¾in (45mm) and a lower flat section made of veneered MDF which was 4⅛in (105mm) high.

TECHNIQUE:

Fitting skirting

Fix the flat section using a level marked line for the top edge, with biscuit marks along it. The joiner is inverted and held against the panelling and the slots made – care is needed as this is working freehand to a line on a vertical surface and anti-slip devices need to be in use. Cut the flat section square at the ends since the lack of mitres won't show, then slot to match the slots on the panelling. Add glue to the slots only (if a finish has already been applied, glue won't stick to the lacquer), biscuit the flat strip on and leave to dry.

Now biscuit downwards into the top edge of the flat strip. Mitre the top moulding to fit between the panelling and slot the bottom edge to match that on the flat strip (size 10 rather than size 20 biscuits may be needed to avoid penetrating through the profile of the moulding). Now glue and push the moulding down onto the flat strip.

The technique of making skirting in two sections and biscuiting together will work in rooms with normal rather than panelled walls, though you should machine both parts out of situ before the skirting is installed because unlike panelling walls are usually quite uneven, thus preventing the two rows of slots from lining up with each other.

TECHNIQUE:

Skirting

LEFT Freehand slotting into vertical wall panelling requires care and a steady hand, anti-slip grips definitely required!

LEFT Slotting down into flat skirting section is relatively easy.

LEFT The use of a block to protect the top moulded section is necessary to avoid damage when tapping it down.

Part 3:
Projects

3:1 T-square

The T-square is the most basic piece of kit for routing, sawing or jointing. It allows operations across the grain, at precisely 90°, and is quick to make and use.

Cutting list

- Blade   25⅝ × 4⅜ × ⅜in × 1off
  650 × 110 × 9mm × 1off
  MDF or ply

- Cross piece   9⅞ × 1⅞ × ¾in × 1off
  250 × 47 × 19mm × 1off
  softwood PAR

- 1in (25mm) CSK screws, PVA glue

Take a suitable piece of straight-edged MDF or ply, ⅜–½in (9–12mm) thick, with a square end. Glue and screw the piece of prepared softwood flat to the underside and flush with the square end. Check that it is truly at 90° by using an accurate try-square or engineer's square and leave to set. You now have a simple and reliable device for slotting and grooving.

Get used to allowing for the correct amount of offset measurement between the edge of the T-square and the joiner blade; indeed you can mark this offset figure on the T-square for handy reference. If you use a router for biscuit slotting, a ⁵⁄₃₂in (4mm) straight cutter in the router used with the T-square will allow you to make T-joints which are otherwise not possible

LARGE JOINER T-SQUARE
SCALE 1:5

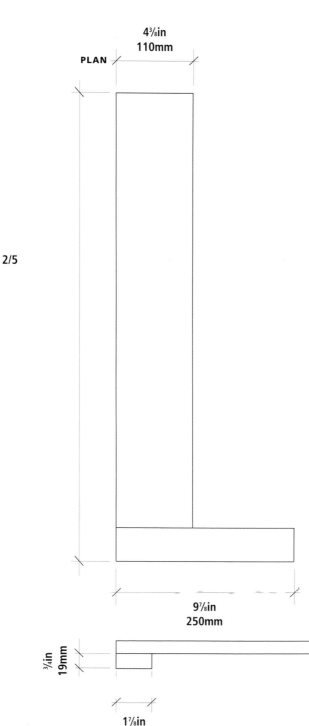

PLAN

4⅜in
110mm

2/5

9⅞in
250mm

¾in
19mm

SIDE

1⅞in
47mm

with a standard router biscuit-cutter set (see chapter 2:4 for more). Always cramp the T-square down rather than being tempted to use hand pressure as a shortcut, as the result would be unpredictable and dangerous. Drill a hanging hole at the far end so it can be stored on the wall near to where you work. The length of the 'blade' is sufficient for a half board width of about 2ft (600mm) but it could be longer or shorter and indeed you may find two different sizes more useful than just one. If you use standard biscuit slotting positions you can mark these on the 'blade' edge to speed up machining even more; thus it doubles as an index stick. The T-square is an essential but very simple gadget, for introducing repetitious accuracy and precision into your work at almost no cost or effort.

ABOVE The completed T-square. It is long enough for 2ft (600mm) wide panels but it can be made longer or shorter.

RIGHT A T-square being used to make shelf slots for a cupboard carcass.

3:2 L-jig

After the T-square, an L-jig is the next most useful device. The illustration shows a typical size with two different width facings but you can make it any size you want. A reference board with a lip (a bench hook, in other words) makes it a complete unit.

Cutting list

L-jig

- Bracket   6 × 6in × 1off
  150 × 150mm × 1off
  (corner to be cut off)

- Facing piece   9⅞ × 6in × 1off
  250 × 150mm × 1off

- Base   11⅛ × 6in × 1off
  282 × 150mm × 1off

Bench hook

- Reference surface   17¾ × 15¾in × 1off
  450 × 400mm × 1off

- Edge piece   15¾ × 2in × 1off
  400 × 50mm × 1off

- All components made from ⅝in (18mm) MDF or ply

- 1¾in (45mm) twinfast screws, PVA glue

ABOVE A narrow L-jig screwed to large flat bench hook. A wider sub-face can be fixed to the L-jig if required.

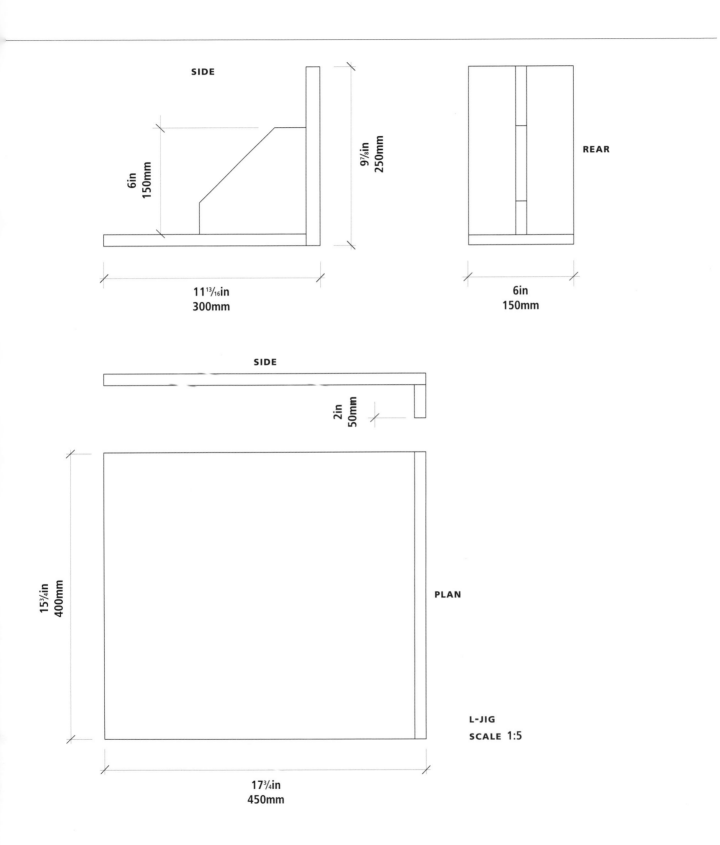

SIDE

6in
150mm

9⅞in
250mm

11¹³/₁₆in
300mm

REAR

6in
150mm

SIDE

2in
50mm

15¾in
400mm

PLAN

L-JIG
SCALE 1:5

17¾in
450mm

3:2 L-jig

ABOVE **The rear of the L-jig.**

Since MDF is the usual construction material, it is cheap enough to make a new L-jig when the old one get too damaged – by screws etc – to keep using it. The bracket needs to be exactly at 90° for the L-jig to be really accurate. It is possible to cut out all the parts using your biscuit joiner in saw mode plus your newly made T-square. It is important to pre-drill fixing holes in MDF as the face is hard to screw through, even with modern self-drilling twinfast screws. Edge screwing makes MDF 'puff out', making it weak and creating bulges that will affect accuracy. Once assembled check for square. The principle of presenting the joiner to the workpiece is a simple but effective one.

ABOVE **Pre-drilling MDF before screwing together is important to avoid it puffing out and splitting.**

LEFT Check for square once assembled.

LEFT Showing how the joiner faces the L-jig and workpiece.

3:3 Biscuit joiner storage case

At least one manufacturer supplies their top-of-the-range model in a wooden case which is sadly just finger-jointed, not biscuited together. Here is a case-making project using ⅜in (9mm)-thick MDF although if you can get hold of some thin prepared solid wood or ply you could use that instead. This case looks simple, which in essence it is, but I should warn you now that some mental juggling is required in order to make the joints all line up as required. In fact this demonstrates several techniques that have already been discussed: sawing; biscuiting thin material; T-joints; the use of packers, and L-jig, index stick and reference surface. If you can master this project it will fit you for doing more complex, large-scale carcass work.

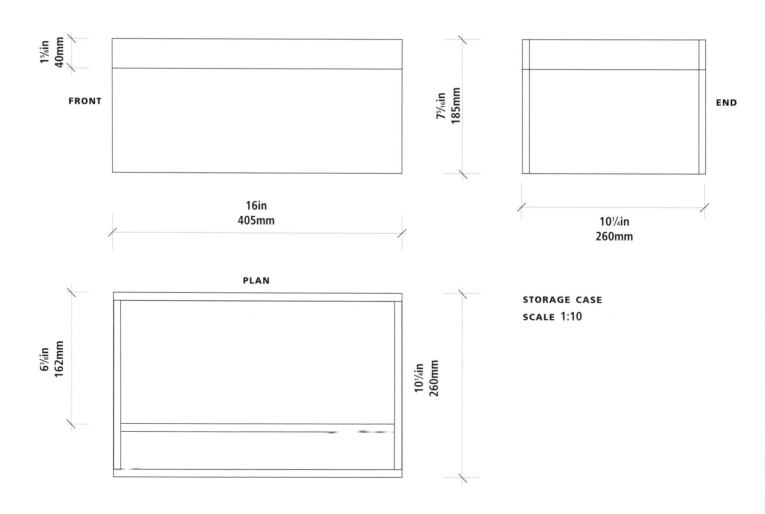

FRONT

1⅝in
40mm

16in
405mm

7⁵⁄₁₆in
185mm

END

10¼in
260mm

PLAN

6³⁄₈in
162mm

10¼in
260mm

STORAGE CASE
SCALE 1:10

Cutting list

Joiner case

• Base	15¼ × 9½in × 1off	
	387 × 242mm × 1off	
• Top	16 × 10¼in × 1off	
	405 × 260mm × 1off	
• Front / Back	16 × 7in × 2off	
	405 × 176mm × 2off	
• Ends	9½ × 7in × 1off	
	242 × 176mm × 1off	
• Divider	15¼ × 5⅛in × 1off	
	387 × 130mm × 1off	

- All components made from ⅜in (9mm) MDF or good quality ply
- 0 size biscuits, PVA glue, case handle, 2 × small brass hinges, 2 × small case catches, 8 × pressed steel case corners, ⅜–½ × ⅛in dia. (10–13 × 3mm dia.) CSK screws

Cut out the front, back and the ends according to the cutting list. Mark out the two biscuit slots per end of front and back components, and faces at each end of the end components using an index stick for uniformity. Bear in mind that the base is fitted inside these pieces for strength but the top sits right over them. The ends 'cap' the front and back, thus preventing the joints from opening under the strain of the lid being pushed back.

Use an L-jig to slot the ends using a ³⁄₁₆in (4mm) packer under the jig and protruding enough to support the components but leaving the biscuit joiner sitting only on the reference surface. This should ensure the slot is positioned slightly to the inside of the finished box for strength, but check on a test piece first and if necessary alter the packers to suit. Then do the slots in the front and back components, again using a ³⁄₁₆in (4mm) packer under the components to position the slot to match the ends.

Dry assemble these pieces (using size 0 biscuits throughout) to give the finished box size and measure and cut a base piece that exactly fits the internal base area using the joiner as a saw. Mark all slot positions with a new index stick, disassemble and slot all components using the ³⁄₁₆in (4mm) packer as before.

Reassemble and cut a division piece that will keep accessories and biscuits away from the joiner. It needs to be no higher than the lower part of the box when the lid has been sawn off. Mark where it needs to be, disassemble the box again and mark out its position properly, nominating which is the face side (this should be on the joiner side of the division as there is more room for the T-square to sit accurately) and mark the biscuit positions. This piece needs a ³⁄₁₆in (4mm) offset too but because it is a T-joint, packers aren't an option for slotting the base and ends. Instead mark back ³⁄₁₆in (4mm) from the face (datum) line, place a T-square against

3:3 Biscuit joiner storage case

the new marks and slot as before. Slot the divider as well using the ³⁄₁₆in (4mm) packer method and reassemble.

ABOVE ³⁄₁₆in (4mm) packer in place under both the L-jig and workpiece.

Repeating these dry assemblies allows you to see how it is going together and ensures that the component sizes will be right. I chose to use biscuit positions at the divider ends which are the same as the box corners. This means the top biscuits are part exposed and need to be chiselled flush but I like the idea of half a biscuit holding the top corner of the divider firmly.

The last piece is the lid which looks neater covering the entire box top. The same marking and slotting method is needed, using an index stick and a ³⁄₁₆in (4mm) offset as before. Fit the lid and check all is well. Take it all apart, glue, cramp and leave to set after wiping off surplus glue with a damp cloth.

ABOVE ³⁄₁₆in (4mm) packer in place with the components lying flat.

Once dry remove the cramps and put the box on edge in a vice. Set the joiner to cut right through the ⅜in (9mm) thickness and the fence to cut the lid part off at the right height. Proceed to saw each face completely. On the last side a ⁵⁄₃₂in (4mm) packer may be required in the previous saw cut so it is packed while held in the vice. The lid should now separate cleanly. Lightly sand the exposed edges and clean up any dry glue runs inside. Sand the exterior and take off the sharpness of the edges and corners. Fit a pair of box hinges, catches and a suitable handle; reinforced corners can be added if required. Now put your prized biscuit joiner and extras in their respective places!

ABOVE Mid-panel joint slotting. Note 4mm offset of T-square from datum line.

ABOVE Final dry assembly to check fit.

3:3 Biscuit joiner storage case

ABOVE Cutting the lid off.

LEFT Finished case.

RIGHT Case open showing interior.

3:4 Joiner working table

I said right at the beginning of the book that the joiner was ideal as a freehand tool and it is; however, static working has a lot to commend it. Since a router can sit in a router table why not have some kind of table for the joiner? I haven't seen one shown anywhere else so I think this may be a bit of a first. It is intended for large panel work such as kitchen cabinets, wardrobes and long workpieces.

The first essential is a strong, reliable flat surface; secondly it needs to be large enough to take panels or long pieces of moulding; and thirdly, it needs some kind of vertical fence for holding components against and a means of clamping them. In addition it is useful to be able to fix the joiner down, such as when jointing narrow components. Unfortunately, this function doesn't fit in so well with the others as it involves damaging the table with screws so some care is needed if the joiner is fixed down. The box section is very rigid and the table can be fixed onto a workmate and stored on end when not in use. The fence can be removed and used with clamps; end stops can be fitted for drawer side slotting and so on.

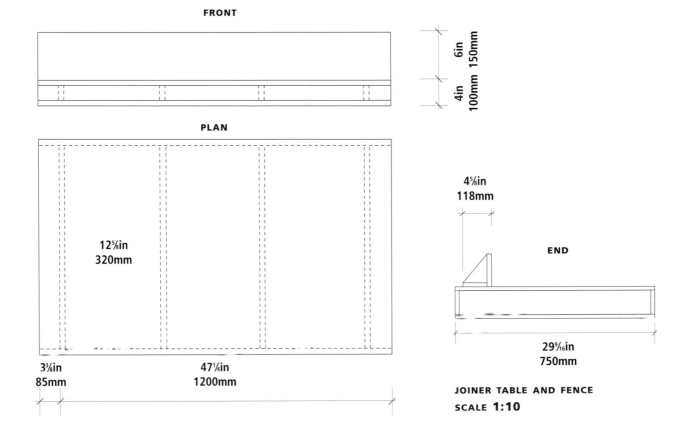

FRONT

6in
150mm

4in
100mm

PLAN

12⅝in
320mm

3⅜in
85mm

47¼in
1200mm

4⅝in
118mm

END

29⁹⁄₁₆in
750mm

JOINER TABLE AND FENCE
SCALE 1:10

Cutting list

Table

- Top / Bottom   47¼ × 29⁹⁄₁₆in × 2off
               1200 × 750mm × 2off

- Front / Back   47¼ × 2¹⁷⁄₃₂in × 2off
               1200 × 64mm × 2off

- Divisions   28⅛ × 2¹⁷⁄₃₂in × 4off
               714 × 64mm × 4off

Fence

- Face   47¼ × 6in × 1off
               1200 × 150mm × 1off

- Base   47¼ × 4in × 1off
               1200 × 100mm × 1off

- Angle pieces cut from scrap to fit L-shape of fence × 4off

- All components made from ⅝in (18mm) MDF

- Size 20 biscuits, PVA glue

- Two small G-cramps required to hold fence in position when operational

- Cramps or heavy weights required for assembly

As with all the projects in this book the dimensions can be varied to suit your circumstances and it isn't necessary to stick to the sizes I have used. However for convenience, and especially as a cutting list is provided, you may prefer to keep to these sizes. The table size is rather wide for its length, longer would be better but it then becomes very heavy and unwieldy and the width is more useful if you are edge-jointing up to half normal board width – about 2ft (600mm).

ABOVE The completed table, ready for its drop box (project 3:5).

3:4 Joiner working table

Although heavy it can be stored up against a wall without taking up much room. The table is just 4in (100mm) thick with divisions to support and stabilize the top and bottom boards making them flat and true, and it is therefore an ideal reference table. The 4in (100mm) overall thickness also allows cramps to be used easily when cramping down the fence or workpieces, and the end divisions are set in anyway allowing the use of small cramps if necessary. This table needs some kind of sturdy base – the drop box in the next chapter is ideal but you can use a couple of trestles or a large workmate so long as it is securely fixed to it. The fence stands 6in (150mm) high

ABOVE Care in marking ensures all components are slotted to match with each other.

reflecting the fact that vertical work support must be adequate, especially with longer workpieces that would otherwise be difficult to hold. Extraction isn't an issue since the joiner is extracted directly, although it is linked to the drop box if that is part of the set up.

Start by cutting out the top and bottom boards from a ⅝in (18mm) sheet of MDF (or decent ply) using the joiner in saw mode or a circular saw with a good quality fine-tooth TCT blade. Because the board size required is large, your T-square will not be adequate; instead measure from the board edges in both directions and carefully mark out allowing for the joiner's blade-to-baseplate offset distance. Manufactured board is cut properly square so you will get reliably sized boards, although the edges may be a bit rough or chewed up because of transport damage. If this is so, make your sizes a bit bigger with the intention of sawing several millimetres off the bad edges afterwards to clean them up and get back to the correct sizes.

Now saw several narrow strips which can be cross-cut to length for the back and front of the table and the four divisions. While you are at it cut the fence parts too – this procedure of accurate pre-cutting of all major parts is standard practice in the trade and it is wise to learn this for yourself, as there is a discipline involved in cutting out economically and accurately, which is essential for good woodworking. Cross-cutting these narrow pieces can be done with the joiner and T-square.

Make up an index stick with strike marks based on the length of the table. Work out all the biscuiting positions by dividing the distance between the two outer strike marks so you end up with roughly 7⅞in

(200mm) spacing; use a calculator for exactness and a steel tape rule to mark it out. Place all the strike marks along the long edges, including the fence pieces. Make up another index stick for the divisions and mark all these up, and then the top and bottom boards after having first carefully marked on the boards where the divisions will fit. Always indicate which side of the pencil line your division is to be placed to avoid problems later.

ABOVE The box section is immensely strong.

3:4 Joiner working table

Make up a dry assembly of the table with some assistance if necessary. If all the biscuits look as if they will close properly, take it apart and glue up. Tap the biscuited joints together with a hammer and a block (to avoid damaging the board) and cramp at alternate biscuit positions. After a while move the cramps along to ensure all the biscuits have a chance to close up tight.

The fence needs four right-angle brackets, which can be sawn from offcuts. Mark their position accurately on the long fence boards, place the strike marks, and cut the biscuit slots. Glue, assemble and cramp the fence, checking it is a true 90°, and leave to dry. For some operations it can be useful to have a low fence, such as a straight square piece of prepared 3 x 2 in (75 x 50mm) softwood, as well as the high MDF one. For drawer box making or similar operations, just cramp two vertical strips to the fence to hold the workpiece tightly in between and push the joiner against it. This table is not meant for using the joiner fixed down as it will damage the surface in the process. If you need to do this, a specially chosen board just a bit bigger than the joiner and the intended components is best.

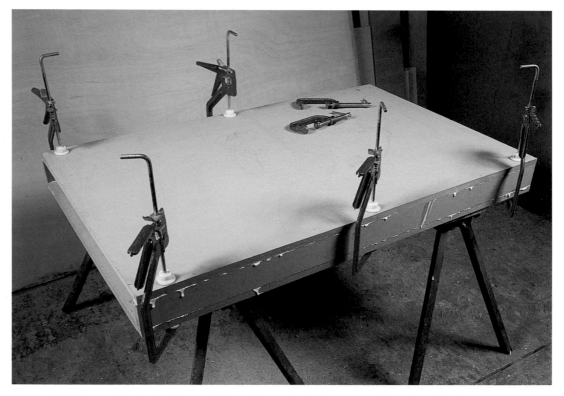

ABOVE The box section is glued up and the surfaces checked to ensure there is no bowing.

ABOVE Cramp the L-fence bracket before attempting to slot it.

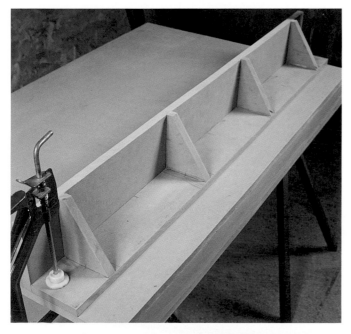

ABOVE An L-fence is used for screwing jigs to or cramping components to it ready to machine.

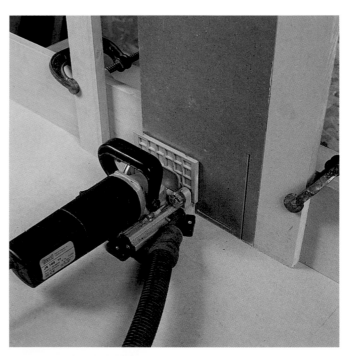

ABOVE Using the table for drawer box work.

3:5 Dust collection drop box

Early on in chapter 1:1 when we looked at the various features of the joiner, I made a strong comment about the necessity of dust extraction. If you use the joiner table you could add this drop box underneath, thus creating a base for it and a means of collecting the bulk of the dust and chippings. A drop box is a collector fitted in the vacuum pipe between the power tool and the extractor providing the suction. For it to work the box must be properly sealed. Biscuit jointing the box together will not be enough – you'll need to run a line of silicone mastic along all the internal joints. The door for emptying needs a rubber weatherseal all round and must be properly latched closed.

Cutting list

- Front / Back   28½ × 23⅝in × 2off
  (712 × 600mm × 2off)

- Ends   28½ × 19in × 2off
  (712 × 482mm × 2off)

- Top / Bottom   23 × 19in × 2off
  (582 × 482mm × 2off)

- All components made from ⅜in (9mm) MDF

- SIze 0 biscuits, PVA glue, 2 × brass hinges, rubber 'P' seal, small CSK screws for hinges, 2 × larger screws for door toggles, mastic and gun for sealing joints, epoxy resin glue

- Plenty of sash or board cramps required for assembly

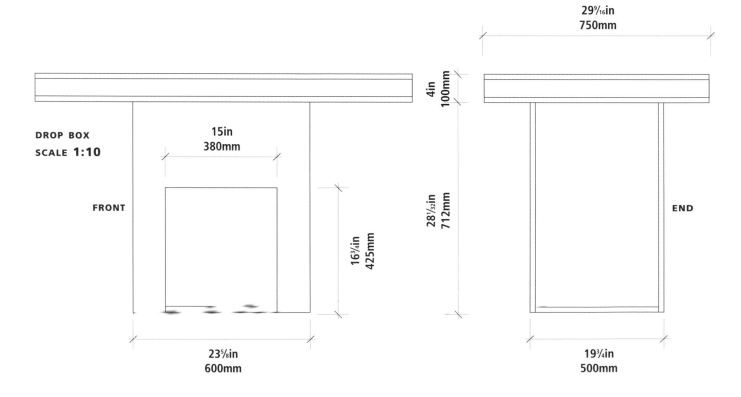

DROP BOX
SCALE **1:10**

FRONT

15in
380mm

16¾in
425mm

23⅝in
600mm

29⁹⁄₁₆in
750mm

4in
100mm

28¹⁄₃₂in
712mm

END

19¾in
500mm

Cut all six panels for the top, bottom, front, back and sides. Lie them down together in their respective positions ensuring all edges have matching letter marking: A to A, B to B and so on; this means you can quickly identify which edges of which components go together, thus avoiding difficulties getting biscuit slots to match. You can then mark straight across the components, allowing for the fact that the front and back are wider than the top and bottom by two board material thicknesses. This marking across technique can and should be used on any carcass work:

professionals regularly mark up their work in this way because it avoids mistakes. To make it consistent though, you should use an index stick for exact repetition accuracy. The front panel should now have the door shape marked on it.

Having marked on one side, rather than turning everything over and re-marking everything before doing the biscuit slots, it is easier to machine with just the existing marks visible and only *then* turn everything over. The net result is that the carcass outside is inside and vice versa, but since

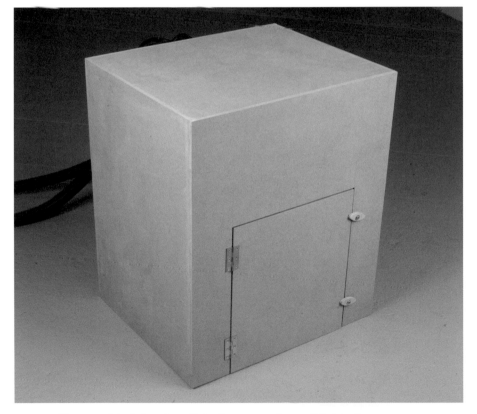

ABOVE The completed drop box. Note the vacuum hoses fitted in the rear.

3:5 Dust collection drop box

your markings are consistent throughout
this does not matter. The only thing you
need to do for the other side is make a
rough mark where the door will be. That
is because at the bottom of the front panel
only one biscuit is required either side of
the door (you do not want a line of
unnecessary biscuits!).

Because only thin board is needed for
the drop box, it is necessary to use packers
to raise the components so the slots are
reasonably centred. Do a dry assembly to
check it all goes together, then glue and
cramp, using plenty of cramps, and swap
them around after a while to ensure all

joints close properly and leave to dry.
Clean off glue runs and sand all joints
smooth.

Re-mark the door shape accurately and
mark outside the door shape with the
blade-to-base offset distance that is correct
for your particular joiner model. Then
clamp a straightedge on the offset marks
and saw along to the next pencil line.
Move the straightedge to the adjoining
pencil line and repeat the cut until you
have cut around all three sides of what
will be the door. Use a padsaw, or better
still a pullsaw to separate the door panel
and clean up the corners.

ABOVE The front panel marked and biscuit slotted, showing the
door shape. This face will end up inside the box, not outside.

ABOVE A clamp-on straightedge being used as a guide for
sawing the door out.

ABOVE Rubber 'P' seal forming an airtight seal when the door is closed.

Glue and cramp strips of MDF under all the three cut edges to act as a rebate for the door to close against. Stick rubber 'P' seal weatherstrip all around the door to create a proper airtight seal.

Seal all carcass joints inside with mastic and use a power drill and a large diameter flatbit to make holes for the in and out pipes on the back of the drop box. Glue the pipes in place using epoxy resin or a tough bonding mastic for a really solid fit. Fit the door hinges; a nice little touch is to use two size 20 biscuits glued together for each of the toggles which hold the door

closed. Note that the door will stand slightly proud because of the weatherseal.

In order to fix the joiner table to the drop box the best method is to invert the table with the drop box dead centre and mark around it. Take the box away and biscuit some pre-drilled strips of wood in place around the pencil-marked rectangle. Now set the whole thing up so the table will fit positively onto the drop box and run some screws through holes in the box to keep the table fixed on. It won't take long to unscrew the table for storage.

3:5 Dust collection drop box

For use, an extractor is attached to the box via one of the pipes, and the joiner via the other, using some flexible extraction hose which can be obtained from a good tool dealer. When you are machining, large chippings are drawn into the drop box and settle there, which means the extractor takes a lot longer to fill up. If you are lucky enough to have an auto sensing extractor it will only come on when you

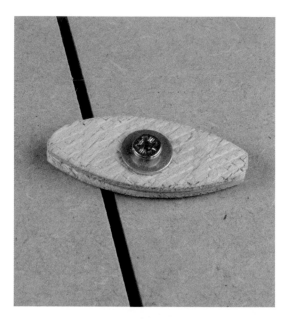

RIGHT The two biscuits for the toggle are glued together with the diagonal grain running in opposing directions for strength.

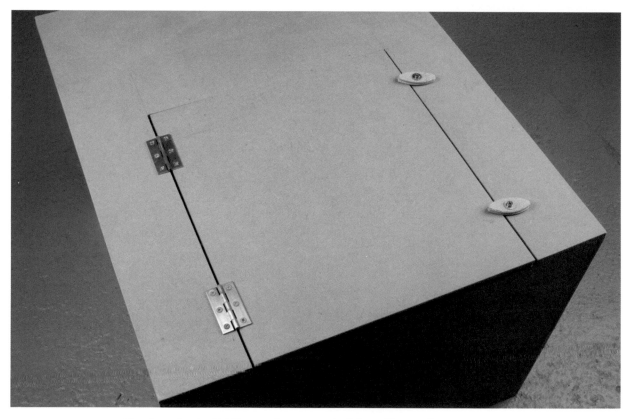

ABOVE The door stands slightly proud on account of the rubber seal.

switch the joiner on. However, the delay time for the extractor to switch itself off should be adjusted on the setting dial because of the extra pipework, which means the dust takes longer to reach the extractor. The table and drop box combination give the serious biscuit-jointing woodworker a good and accurate working setup that can also be used for setting out and assembly work.

ⓚKEY POINT

When emptying both the drop box and the extractor remember to wear a dust mask. This also applies when sweeping up in the workshop. Otherwise all your care in dust removal will be undone as you are exposed to large quantities of very fine hazardous dust.

ⓚKEY POINT

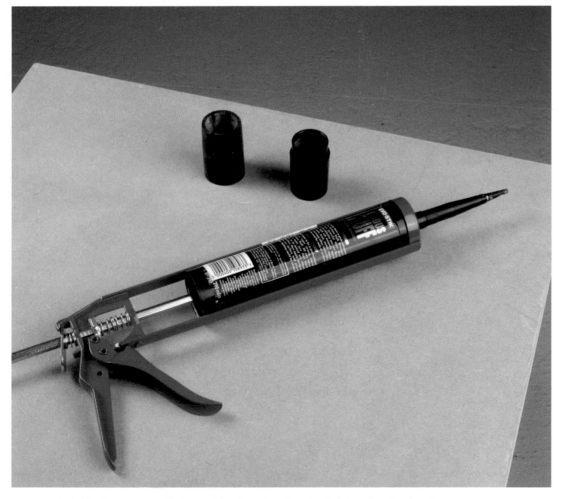

ABOVE **A rigid glue-type mastic is used for bonding the pipe inlet and outlet in place.**

Glossary

A

Aliphatic resin glue
'High tack rate' glue for rapid initial bonding.

Arbor
The spindle on which a blade or cutter is mounted.

Architrave
Moulding applied around a doorway.

Auto sensing
Electronic circuit on a vacuum extractor that switches on when a power tool is used.

B

Bead
A half-round shape.

Brushes
Gaphite carbon blocks which transmit electricity to rotating commutator.

Bullnose
Traditional moulding profile.

C

Cabinetmaking
The construction of furniture.

Carpentry
Applying sawn and prepared timber to buildings.

Commutator
Sectioned collar on motor spindle to which each winding is separately connected.

Cornice
A moulding overhanging the top of a piece of furniture.

D

Dado
A moulding low on a wall to protect it from furniture and to mark a break in the decor.

Drop box
Container connected between a power tool and extractor to collect heavy chippings.

F

Face and edge (UK)
Denotes the two best adjoining surfaces on prepared wood – marked by pencil.

Face moulding
Moulding cut into the front surface of the wood.

Fall-front
Front face of joiner which swings down and can be set at various angles.

Fixed-front
A fixed-front face on the joiner.

G

Grain
Simplistic description of the face structure of wood.

H

HP
Horsepower, a measure of energy produced at the tool spindle or shaft.

HPLV
High pressure, low volume; a small vacuum cleaner-type extractor.

HSE
Health and Safety Executive, the UK agency responsible for safety in industry.

HSS
High speed steel, an alloy of steel superior to plain carbon steel for toolmaking applications.

HVLP
High volume, low pressure; a large industrial extraction machine.

J

Joiner (US); Jointer (UK)
Term for a biscuit-jointing machine.

Joinery (UK)
Making of wood components to be fitted in buildings.

Joinery (US)
Making of all furniture and fittings.

K

Kerf
The slot created by a sawblade.

L

Lamb's tongue
Aptly named traditional moulding profile.

M

MDF
Medium density fibreboard, made with compressed wood fibre and resin.

Micron
Unit of measure used to describe small particles, especially the dust from wood.

Motor winding
One of a series of varnished copper electrical wires spun around a steel core.

O
Ogee
A classical moulding consisting of a concave and a convex form.

P
PAR
'Prepared all round', timber that is planed on all four surfaces.

PVA
Polyvinyl acetate, a cheap reliable glue for ordinary use.

Per cube foot (UK)
How hardwoods are still sold in the UK.

Per metre run (UK)
How softwood is sold.

Picture rail
A revived moulding, high up on a wall, for hanging picture frames.

Planted moulding
A moulding applied to existing woodwork.

Polyurethane glue
Foams slightly on application, sets quickly, works on wet wood.

Pre-scoring
A very shallow cut to slice wood fibres, thus preventing tearout when deep cutting.

R
Roller stands
Supports for wood as it enters and leaves a machine table.

Router
A portable power tool with a high-speed motor for machining joints and mouldings.

S
Sawn timber
Timber that has been cut into usable sections but requires proper planing for use.

Sealed bearings
Superior to ordinary ballraces. Designed for high speed and keeping dust out.

Skirting
Large moulded strip that decorates and finishes a wall where it meets the floor.

Spline
Term for a biscuit (also known as a plate or flat dowel).

Strike mark
Pencil mark across two components to show where to biscuit.

Superglue
Contains cyanoacrylate, useful for instant minor wood repairs.

T
TCT
Tungsten carbide, a metal alloy for cutting abrasive materials including man-made boards.

Tearout
Torn wood fibres especially across the grain. Also known as breakout.

Timber (UK); Lumber (US)
Felled trees, partly converted or unconverted for use.

Torus top
Skirting top moulding featuring a half-round shape.

Tufnol
Industrial sheet material suitable for jigmaking.

Twinfast
Type of modern screw with a parallel shank and two driving threads.

U
Urea formaldehyde glue
Sets hard and is gap filling (Extramite brand in UK).

V
Veneer
Wafer-thin sheet of wood usually glued to a board.

Veneer pins
Tiny pins, thinner than panel pins, useful for neat, split-free fixing.

W
Watts
Expression of a machine's electrical consumption and output.

Manufacturers

AEG
Worldwide distribution
www.aeg-pt.com

Axminster
www.axminster.co.uk Products are
not currently available to the US

Bosch
UK: www.bosch.co.uk
USA: www.boschtools.com

Clarke
UK: www.clarkeinternational.com
USA: www.clarkeusa.com

DeWalt
UK: www.dewalt.co.uk
USA: www.dewalt.com

Draper
UK: www.drapertools.com
Available to US customers from
JustOffBase,
Unit 1 Harlequin Business Park,
Kenny Hill, Bury St Edmunds,
Suffolk IP28 8DS, UK

Ferm
Worldwide distribution
www.ferm.com

Freud
Worldwide distribution
www.freudtools.com

Lamello
Worldwide distribution
www.lamello.com

Mafelll
Europe: www.mafell.de
USA: www.mafell.com

Makita
Worldwide distribution
www.makita.com

Milwaukee
Europe: www.milwaukee-et.com
USA: www.milwaukeetool.com

Porter Cable
UK: www.porter-cable.uk.com
USA: www.porter-cable.com

Rexon
UK: www.rexon.co.uk
USA: www.tradesman-rexon.com

SIP
Worldwide distribution
www.sip-group.com

Skil
Worldwide distribution
www.skil.com

Trend
UK: www.trendmachinery.co.uk
USA: www.trend-usa.com

Virutex
Europe: www.virutex.es
USA: www.virutex.com

Measurements

Although care has been taken to ensure that the imperial measurements are true and accurate, they are only conversions from metric; they have been rounded up or down to the nearest convenient equivalent in cases where the metric measurements themselves are only approximate. When following the projects, use either the metric or the imperial measurements; do not mix units.

Index

About the author

Anthony Bailey has had several career changes which have channelled his skills firmly in the direction of woodworking. Originally trained and later employed as a professional photographer, he has also worked as a furniture restorer, cabinet-maker and set builder. As well as performing as a demonstrator at several woodworking shows, he has written for various woodworking magazines and is the author of *Routing for Beginners*, a best-seller that has subsequently been reprinted as a revised and expanded edition.

Guild of Master Craftsman Publications,
Castle Place, 166 High Street, Lewes,
East Sussex BN7 1XU, United Kingdom

Tel: 01273 488005 Fax: 01273 402866
Website: www.gmcbooks.com

Contact us for a complete catalogue, or visit our website.
Orders by credit card are accepted.